A Modest Proposal

Students Can Learn

John E. Roueche

in collaboration with

John C. Pitman

A MODEST PROPOSAL

Students Can Learn

Jossey-Bass Inc., Publishers
San Francisco · Washington · London · 1972

A MODEST PROPOSAL: STUDENTS CAN LEARN
by John E. Roueche, in collaboration with John C. Pitman

Published in Great Britain by
Jossey-Bass, Inc., Publishers
St. George's House
44 Hatton Garden, London E.C.1

Library of Congress Catalogue Card Number LC 73-184956

International Standard Book Number ISBN 0-87589-116-0

Manufactured in the United States of America

JACKET DESIGN BY WILLI BAUM

FIRST EDITION

Code 7201

The Jossey-Bass
Series in Higher Education

JOHN E. ROUECHE

The University of Texas

Consulting Editor, Community and Junior Colleges

FOR ALLAN S. HURLBURT

Preface

A Modest Proposal: Students Can Learn is intended to facilitate instructional change. It is neither a how-to-do-it manual nor a compendium of theoretical research. We have selected a theoretical base which we believe will further educational change in directions which are important and necessary. We have also selected operational alternatives which have shown their value in community colleges with which we have been associated. This work, then, is a combination of theory and practice, organized with a consistent rationale and directed at facilitating a particular change.

The specific focus of this book is community-college teachers, administrators, and counselors. Personnel entering community colleges often fail to understand the mission of these colleges and the diverse range of students who enroll there. Also, many community-college faculty and staff need help in devising effective teaching, counseling, and administering strategies so that they may improve their service to their institutions and students.

Teachers and administrators frequently ask why teacher-preparation institutions or education departments do not inform them of techniques to help them meet the broad range of student interests and abilities. They also ask how they can reeducate in-service personnel to do a better job than they presently are doing and to do it within realistic time limits.

These questions present two major problems. First, current communication is poor between professors who train community-college personnel and the researchers and product developers who provide the tools for such training. Recent (three to five years) research and products should be incorporated into training practices. Education has experienced an explosion of knowledge in the past decade. Often, researchers and product developers are unaware of what the other is doing. The results of the effectiveness of instructional products are not circulated so that others can build upon them. Even at the research and product-development level the wheel is sometimes reinvented. This book attempts to consolidate some of the most compelling recent research and product developments to show how they may be implemented.

The second major problem we wish to deal with is the lack of an overall strategy for total institutional change and development. A visit to typical community colleges reveals that they are instituting or about to institute many changes encompassing all aspects of their operations—teaching, counseling, administration, governance, student relations, community action, extension, and so on. Yet, if the visitor talks with personnel from the major divisions of a college, he is likely to discover that one division or department often has little understanding of what other divisions and departments are doing. Duplication of effort, cross-purposes, and inconsistent use of terminology slow the progress of institutional change. Institutional purposes or goals are typically confusing or even nonexistent. A major national study by Garrison (1969) showed that one of the most frequent complaints of teachers was that they did not know what the goals of their institutions were.

Institutional change requires comprehensive planning in all major areas of the two-year college. This book is designed to show those who are concerned with such institutional planning how they can operate in a college committed to implementing the open-door policy. The first step in planning a change is establishing clear goals.

Preface

Where does the college want to go? Once the goals are set, strategies for attaining them can be developed. Finally, some evaluation must be carried on so that everyone knows where he stands and what he needs to do to improve his strategies. How to accomplish these goals in a systematic manner constitutes the practical portion of the book.

Chapter One reviews the general purposes of the community college. It also considers shortcomings and strong points in terms of the stated goals of the colleges.

Chapter Two is an elaboration of a philosophical teaching and learning base more general, we feel, than the ones now generally employed. We contend that the present philosophical base in most community colleges either is poorly defined or is ignored. General statements of purpose are usually consistent with national goals (to provide two years of post secondary-school education to all Americans); however, the operation of many community colleges is inconsistent with such general statements. A carefully considered value base which ties operational principles to general statements of purpose helps eliminate contradictions and aids faculty and staff in developing a clear statement of goals.

Chapter Three examines learning research. This brief review is not intended to be an exhaustive examination of the major ideas of learning theorists. Our purpose is to show that our philosophical base is supported by learning theory. We also attempt to relate our philosophical base to the later practical development of our system. The reader may consider this chapter a link between our new value base and our program for implementing the strategies needed to bring about change.

Chapter Four discusses several systematic approaches to instructional and institutional change. We follow these with our own approach—an eclectic construct.

Chapter Five combines the theoretical with the practical. We first explore Benjamin Bloom's mastery learning thesis at length. Bloom argues that all, or almost all, students can master material if given enough time. Bloom's idea is central to the philosophical base we have elaborated—that each individual can realize his creative potential. This idea is revolutionary. Consequently, we devote the last portion of the chapter to a detailed consideration of the practical implications of Bloom's concepts for key staff and faculty in the community college.

In Chapter Six we take a straightforward how-do-I-do-it approach. The need has been identified, and the theory has been developed. Now the reader wants concrete information and examples of how a systematic approach to instructional and institutional change can be implemented. This final chapter, although a discrete unit in the book, should be considered only the external or observable product which embodies larger values and philosophical commitments. An analogy may help illustrate this point. A boat—a twenty-foot sloop—is a product which can be built with the proper tools and detailed, step-by-step building instructions. Yet, to most owners, constructing the product is only a small part of the story. What one can do with that boat—take off for Tahiti or simply to a pleasant island in the bay—is far more important and satisfying. Also, how one feels about the boat—it may represent freedom, excitement, or contentment—is a vital part of the definition of the product. We hope that at the end of reading this book you will be able to build your own "boat" if you desire to do so. We hope you will also have some glimpses of what you may do with such a "boat" and vicariously share some of our deep feelings about it.

We could not possibly mention everyone who has contributed to our thoughts in developing this book. However, we do want to acknowledge the contributions of those colleagues who assisted our work in major ways. Several community-college presidents operate institutions that approximate the model we have developed, and they have contributed both documents and ideas. Our thanks to Robert Zimmer, president, Passaic County Community College (New Jersey); Ervin Harlacher, president, Brookdale Community College (New Jersey); Robert Turner, president, Moraine Valley Community College (Illinois); Robert Lahti, president, William Rainey Harper College (Illinois); Richard Hagemeyer, president, Central Piedmont Community College (North Carolina); Donald

Preface

Rippey, president, El Centro College (Texas); Robert Clinton, president, Western Texas College (Texas); Dudley Boyce, president, Golden West College (California); Morton Shanberg, president, Hillsborough Junior College (Florida); Thomas Cottingham, president, Southeastern Community College (North Carolina); Thomas E. Barton, president, Greenville Technical Institute (South Carolina); Joe B. Rushing, chancellor, Tarrant County Community College District (Texas), and his campus presidents Charles McKinney and Donald Anthony; Fred Taylor, president, College of the Mainland (Texas); and Craven Sumerell, president, Piedmont Technical Institute (North Carolina).

Other colleagues who made special contributions include Gabriel Ofiesh, professor of education, American University (Washington, D.C.); Walter Hunter, associate dean, Meremac Community College, Saint Louis Junior College District (Missouri); Yvonne Pierce, dean of learning resources, Hillsborough Junior College (Florida); Barbara P. Washburn, educational development officer, Mitchell College (North Carolina); Stuart and Rita Johnson, associate professors, Medical College of the University of North Carolina; Kenneth Bradshaw, dean of instruction, Mitchell College (North Carolina); Larnie G. Horton, president, Kittrell Junior College (North Carolina); and Norman Camp, dean, Kittrell Junior College.

We express special thanks and appreciation to our friends who read and reviewed major portions of the manuscript for their suggestions for improvement. In particular we thank Richard E. Wilson, associate executive director, American Association of Junior Colleges; Thomas M. Hatfield, associate commissioner for community colleges, Texas Coordinating Board; B. Lamar Johnson, professor of higher education, University of California, Los Angeles; Barton R. Herrscher, president, Mitchell Junior College (North Carolina); George A. Baker, Richard L. Brownell, John Niblock, and Oscar Mink, all of the National Laboratory for Higher Education, Durham, North Carolina.

We also acknowledge the contributions of Richard Morgan, Mitchell College (North Carolina), who contributed learning units

Preface

which are included in the appendix. Some examples of objectives and learning activities cited in Chapter Six are also from their materials. We are grateful to Westinghouse Learning Corporation for allowing us to include unit samples from Morgan's psychology course.

For manuscript-preparation assistance, we acknowledge the contributions of Francine Lerner, Norma Dickson, Sharon Rigby, Mrs. Sam Rigsbee, Susan Chamberlain, and Judy Frieling.

Without the assistance and advice of our friends and colleagues, this work would not have been possible. For all shortcomings, however, we accept full and final responsibility.

This book is for Nelda, Michelle, and Jay Roueche, and Joyce and Sonya Pitman.

Austin   John E. Roueche
January 1972   John C. Pitman

Contents

xv

Contents

A Modest Proposal

Students Can Learn

1

Failure of
Traditional Roles

The contemporary community college is a manifestation of the dream of offering postsecondary-school education to all. The strength of the community college, often called "democracy's college," lies in its ability to provide education that is responsive to local needs. Students of all races, ages, abilities, interests, and socioeconomic backgrounds may choose from several educational objectives: college transfer work, occupational and technical training programs, or general interest courses. The community college offers something for everyone at minimum expense.

The positive social philosophy of the community college (to provide opportunity for all who seek it) provides a supportive environment to students who might find the atmosphere of traditional four-year institutions difficult to cope with. The phenomenal growth of these colleges demonstrates their appeal.

Universal postsecondary-school education is a great experiment in public education. It goes beyond the general educational

1

goals of transmitting cultural and social values and aspires to provide employment opportunities, increase competence in civic affairs, and help students find educational fulfillment.

Community colleges are the most recently established educational institution. They began in the late 1800s and expanded in numbers soon after the turn of the century. Gleazer (1963, p. 3) describes the community college as the only educational institution that can truly be called an American social invention.

Many regard the establishment of community colleges as the most obvious effort to democratize higher education. Community colleges allow each individual the opportunity to progress as far as his interests and abilities permit. Traditional universities have not shown a willingness or ability to offer educational opportunities for all. These institutions in contrast to community colleges have been geared to students of higher socioeconomic backgrounds with higher levels of achievement. Universities are research-oriented and exist to advance basic knowledge rather than to provide practical training. They serve a necessary educational function, but they have not addressed themselves to the educational needs of the majority of the postsecondary-school students, particularly those who lack the requirements for completing baccalaureate programs. The community college, which offers courses below the collegiate level, is in an excellent position to answer the needs of such nontraditional students (Blocker and others, 1965, p. 268). As liberal arts colleges and universities continue to maintain entrance standards and assume little responsibility for nontraditional students, community colleges, with their open-door policies, will be forced to assume more responsibility. Students who formerly populated remedial courses in four-year institutions are now sitting in community college classrooms (Bossone, 1966, p. 1).

Burgeoning enrollments and continued selective admissions at senior colleges and universities make the open-door policy of community colleges a matter of national necessity and concern. Under the Master Plan for Higher Education in California, university enrollment is now limited to students in the upper eighth of their high school graduating class, and state college enrollment is

2

limited to the upper third. The community college is now the only avenue of public higher education for two-thirds of the high school graduates of California.

The social and economic pressure to extend higher educational opportunity to all is obvious. Bloom (1968, p. 2) observes:

> Some societies need only a small number of highly educated persons in the economy and can provide the economic support for only a small proportion of the students to complete secondary or higher education. Under such conditions much of the effort of the schools and the external examining system is to find ways of rejecting the majority of students at various points in the educational system and to discover the talented few who are to be given advanced educational opportunities. Such societies invest a great deal more in the prediction and selection of talent than in the development of such talent. The complexities of the skills required by the economy in the United States and in other highly developed nations mean that we can no longer operate on the assumption that completion of secondary and advanced education is for the few. Whatever might have been the case previously, highly developed nations must seek to find ways to increase the proportions of the age group that can successfully complete both secondary and higher education. The problem is to determine how the largest proportion of the age group can learn effectively those skills and subject matter regarded as essential for their own development in a complex society.

Increased educational opportunities for all has become a societal demand. Postsecondary-school education is a necessity, not a luxury. The community college offers the best hope for meeting this need. In fact, the community college has already achieved much success in removing geographic, financial, and social barriers to higher education.

The accessibility of institutions of higher learning is a major factor in community college enrollment rates. National studies of the community college indicate that enrollment begins to decline when potential students reside more than fifteen miles from campus and becomes almost nonexistent outside of a thirty-five mile radius. In their study of educational opportunity for youth from disadvantaged backgrounds, Trent and Medsker (1965) compared college attendance rates in sixteen cities which had similar demographic and industrial features but varying public college accessibility. They found that where community colleges existed, a higher proportion of students attended. In such communities, 53 per cent of the high school graduates entered college. This figure was 6 per cent higher than in communities having a state college and 20 per cent higher than in communities with no college.

When Medsker and Trent compared the college attendance rate of high school students in the upper 40 per cent of their senior classes, 82 per cent of the students in upper socioeconomic groups attended college even though there may have been no college in their community. Only 22 per cent of the students from the lower socioeconomic groups, however, went to college if there was no local college available. The Trent-Medsker study suggests that greater college attendance can be expected from lower socioeconomic groups as these institutions become local. Other research studies confirm that "nearness to home" is a primary reason for student attendance at community colleges (Cross, 1968, p. 34; Florida State University Department of Education, 1963, p. 1).

State surveys of higher education in all sections of the country are recommending plans under which community colleges will "cover" the respective states. Massachusetts, Florida, and others have developed plans under which community colleges will be situated within commuting distance of 95 to 99 per cent of the population. California now has community colleges within commuting distance of 85 to 90 per cent of its population.

Until the advent of the community college, college attendance was more dependent upon family income than upon student aptitude or aspirations. Although the research on financial barriers to college attendance is not as conclusive as that for geographical barriers, it is nonetheless convincing. In their report on tuition and fee charges in community colleges, D'Amico and Bokelman (1962, pp. 36–39) found that the public community college had provided educational opportunity to persons who otherwise would not have continued their education beyond high school.

A California study found that of the three systems of public higher education (universities, state colleges, and community colleges), students attending public community colleges were in greatest need. (The term *need* was defined as the cost of education beyond what could be expected from family contributions and the students' summer employment.) This study estimated that 24 per cent of the students planning to enroll in public two-year colleges in 1967–1968 required financial assistance. It pointed out that the typical junior college student is from the lowest income group of those attending college in California. He is least willing or able to borrow and least likely to enter a highly paid occupation that facilitates loan repayment (Coordinating Council for Higher Education, 1967). Studies in Florida support these findings. Twenty-seven per cent of the students in Florida reported cost as a major factor in their decisions to enroll in a public community college rather than a state college or university (Florida State University Department of Education, 1963, p. 2). A review of recent research (Cross, 1968) corroborates the view that community colleges are now serving groups of students for whom finances are a primary concern. Comparisons between community-college students and their senior-college counterparts indicate that the two-year college students are more likely to come from lower socioeconomic backgrounds, work while attending college, and depend upon the low cost of the community college. The community college has played an important role in removing the financial barriers to postsecondary-school education (Cross, 1968). It should be kept in mind, however, that all college fees represent barriers to those who cannot pay the price. Even though the community college is the most economical avenue of higher education, it is still far from free.

In earlier works, motivation has been identified as another barrier to postsecondary-school education (Roueche, 1968). Even if all geographical and financial barriers could be eliminated, racial minorities, women, and the children of parents of low educational and socioeconomic status would still be underrepresented in the college population (Cross, 1969, p. 5). No community college intentionally discriminates on the basis of race, but the doors of many do not swing wide enough to admit those who do not "seek"

5

further education, those who are not "qualified," or those who are not motivated to follow the traditional curriculum.

Many discussions have focused on the open door. How "open" is it? In a study of state master plans, Hurlburt (1969) concluded that the term *open door* is accurate if it is understood to mean that admissions are not competitive. He did conclude, however, that "the one stated limitation is that educational opportunities be made available commensurate with the individual's ability to profit from them. In other words, opportunities should be open, not indiscriminately, but to those who seek them and can benefit from them." The key word is *seek*. Community colleges have long assumed that because their doors were open, their curriculum choices broad, and their tuition costs low, all students "who could profit from instruction" would automatically enroll. In fact, thousands of postsecondary-school students know little, if anything, about community colleges. Some segments of our population simply do not "seek" education beyond high school.

Two-year colleges have done little student recruitment. The open-door policy should include an active effort to identify, recruit, enroll, and retain all potential students. What individual could not "profit" from instruction in some area?

Most thoughtful writers in the community-college field have expressed concern over the fate of increasing numbers of nontraditional students who enter through the open door. The open door is sometimes cynically referred to as the revolving door. One thing is certain—few of the students stay long (Roueche, 1968).

Almost all colleges profess open-door admission policies. However, nontraditional students do not persist long. Therefore philosophy and practice are at odds. The open door must be more than an admissions statement.

Although postsecondary-school educational opportunity for all is not yet a reality, the public community college has exerted more effort to remove educational barriers than has any other institution of higher education. From its genesis, the community college has stressed the need for effective guidance and counseling programs to assist nontraditional students. Community colleges have

6

attempted to provide programs which enable any student to enter college and attain his personal objectives. Currently, remedial, developmental, or compensatory courses enroll more community-college students than do any other courses.

Community-college students have different needs from those of their four-year counterparts. "Poor" students are in the majority. They cut across racial, ethnic, and class lines. The open-door policy produces a heterogeneous student body, representative of the total population. Community colleges must expect and provide for students from the lower two-thirds of the academic spectrum—an important yet frequently ignored fact.

Since the mid-1950s, educators have become increasingly aware of the problems of nontraditional or disadvantaged students in community colleges. Rapidly increasing enrollments have aggravated the problem. Although the disadvantaged students are by no means a homogeneous group, they do have some characteristics in common such as low economic status, low social status, low educational achievement, marginal or no employment, limited participation in community organizations, and limited potential for immediate upward mobility. They include blacks, Mexican-Americans, Puerto Ricans, American Indians, and southern rural or mountain whites. Their culture has failed to provide them with experiences typical of the youth that colleges are accustomed to teaching. Students from these groups have historically enrolled in community colleges, and increasingly greater numbers may be expected to attend community colleges in the future. As a result, student bodies in two-year colleges will become increasingly complex and diverse.

A major misconception about community-college students has developed because educators have failed to recognize that the standards for evaluating success in selective institutions do not apply to community-college students. Too much attention has been given to academic achievement and intelligence as indicators or predictors of student success. Standardized achievement tests and standardized intelligence tests are customarily used in comparing the two-year and four-year students. In such comparisons, community-college students come out second best. The community-college student's

7

composite scores fall well below the scores of the four-year student. Educators then conclude that two-year college students are poorer students. However, the "scholastic aptitude" that is being measured by these tests is the rate of learning rather than the capacity for learning. Community-college students generally learn at slower rates than four-year students, but it is unjustified to conclude that their learning capacity is less.

The term *junior college* has been used historically to refer to open-door postsecondary-school institutions. It is particularly common in California, Texas, and Florida. The term is unfortunate, however, because it lends a qualitative connotation to the institution: junior in the sense of inferior. This usage is inappropriate. As a quantitative measure, the term *junior college* correctly indicates that the college offers fewer than four years of study. In this sense, the word *junior* refers to someone who is younger than his father. Few, however, would say that such a junior is necessarily less worthy than his father.

Using traditional measures of aptitude, both Medsker and Tillery (1971) and Thornton (1966, p. 150) concluded that the average aptitude of junior college students is somewhat below that of four-year college students. Coleman (also using standardized achievement tests) investigated the relative position of black and white high school graduates and found a considerable gap. The same findings would result, although somewhat less pronounced, for other minority groups and poor whites. Coleman (1966, pp. 174–175) concluded:

> These tests do not measure intelligence nor attitudes nor qualities of character. Furthermore they are not, nor are they intended to be, "culture free." Quite the reverse: they are culture bound. What they measure are the skills which are among the most important in our society for getting a good job and moving up to a better one and for full participation in an increasingly technical world. Consequently, a pupil's test scores at the end of public school provide a good measure of the range of opportunities open to him as he finishes school—a wide range of choices of jobs or colleges if these skills are very high; a very narrow range that includes only the most menial jobs if these skills are very low.

8

Failure of Traditional Roles

A comprehensive review of research by Cross (1968) provided the following summary: (1) Very little is known about the pattern of special abilities and aptitudes of the community-college student. Much research is needed to identify patterns of abilities and special skills. (2) As a group, community-college students have a more practical orientation to college and to life than do their more intellectually disposed peers in four-year colleges. (3) Community-college students are not sufficiently sure of themselves to venture into new and untried fields, and they appear to seek more certain pathways to success and financial security. (4) As a group, community-college students are less confident of their academic abilities than are four-year college students. They do express confidence in nonacademic areas. (5) Although 68 per cent of the community-college students come from homes of unskilled, skilled, and semiprofessional workers, nearly two-thirds of them aspire to managerial and professional occupations.

Community colleges have become the primary vehicle for upward social and economic mobility for the lower two-thirds of the population. A large portion of this group brings diverse learning problems to the community college which call for drastic modification of the traditional teaching-learning process. Remedying learning deficiencies must continue to be a major responsibility of the community college if it is to realize its unique mission of providing educational opportunities to all.

The preceding discussion of students is not intended to be exhaustive. Many other factors (age, marital status, employment while in college, recreational differences) could have been mentioned. They further differentiate the community-college student from his four-year counterpart. However, the foregoing discussion does illustrate that community-college students are not traditional students. Hence, they cannot effectively be treated as such.

We have described the two-year college as a unique, multipurpose institution catering to a nontraditional student body. Is its faculty in agreement with this purpose? Unfortunately, many are not. The typical community-college faculty member is, like his colleague in the four-year college, an academic specialist. He derives

9

his greatest satisfaction from transmitting the knowledge of his chosen discipline to able students. Consequently he prefers to teach advanced and specialized courses. These courses afford him the opportunity to teach that which he knows best. Simply stated, some community-college instructors want to teach students who are easy to teach—those who are "already motivated." The old adage that "college is here if you want to take advantage of it" is still prevalent. Instructors in remedial or developmental courses often do not demonstrate any knowledge or understanding of the basic objectives of the courses. The instructor himself often is no more informed than the vague objectives which accompany the course outlines. Many instructors indicate that their primary objective is to bring the student up to the level of the college-credit course (Bossone, 1966, p. 14).

Both community-college and university instructors are concerned about "status" and being properly identified with higher education. Teaching remedial or developmental courses does not identify the instructor with higher academia. In fact, some teachers assert that nontraditional students and special programs are of little or no concern to them. They are more interested in academic rank, tenure, and teacher rights (Medsker and Tillery, 1971, pp. 91–92). This attitude is like that of the family doctor who never took "hard to cure" cases.

The result of this attitude is a ridiculously high attrition rate. Although some teachers appear genuinely concerned, many simply explain attrition as proof that the students were not "college material." Such teacher pessimism tends to be self-fulfilling. In fact, teacher expectations may be the most important simple determinant of student achievement in any classroom (Bloom, 1968). This conclusion is discouraging in light of evidence that not enough qualified instructors can be brought into an effective working force to provide for the learning needs of two-year students. A gap exists between what the community-college instructor views as his role and what his role must be if the institution is to make good on its promise to provide educational opportunity for all (Medsker and Tillery, 1971).

10

Failure of Traditional Roles

The main responsibility of the community-college instructor is teaching. The community college considers itself a teaching institution. The two-year college instructor must, therefore, be committed to teaching and possess a special knowledge of instructional processes (Cohen, 1966, p. 21). Although the community college instructor is not expected to conduct educational research, he should engage in a deliberate effort to help his students learn.

Having a master's degree in a subject area does not ensure that an instructor is a competent teacher. In most cases he knows little about instructional processes. Few instructors have had pedagogical training (Cohen and Brawer, 1968). In fact, preservice faculty training for teaching in community colleges has rarely been available to graduate students. Typically they serve internships in schools other than junior colleges. Friedman (1969, p. 103) sums up this state of unpreparedness: "For most recruits, the public junior college is a new organizational work setting and level for which they usually have had no special or unique preservice preparation."

Educators often imply that innovative teaching methods are being used in community colleges. However, such methods do not develop in the hands of traditional teachers. A study of community-college instructors which included high school teachers, graduate students, and college professors showed that all tended toward the lecture method—especially the group recruited from high school (Friedman, 1969, p. 107).

Two-year–college programs follow many directions. Transfer programs vary little from college to college because they reflect the requirements of the four-year institutions. The sequence of courses tends to be set. Although the four-year colleges are demonstrating a growing willingness to accept diversity in such programs, many community colleges show little inclination to modify their programs. Even though they are aware of the nontraditional nature of their students, many colleges are still unwilling to abandon traditional undergraduate programs.

Transfer students do well after they transfer (Willingham and Findikgan, 1969). Knoell and Medsker (1966, p. 19) conclude

11

that, "on the whole, the junior college transfers were very well satisfied with their experience in the junior college and encountered few serious problems in the four-year institutions." Yet, Medsker and Tillery (1971) found that only one-third of those starting transfer progams in the two-year colleges actually transferred. In view of this drop-out rate, community colleges cannot claim great success in the transfer area. We contend that many "average," high-ability students who might have continued were stifled by traditional teaching patterns.

In the occupational field, however, the community colleges offer considerable diversity. The students may choose short (six months to a year) training or retraining programs in a skill requiring relatively little abstract ability or technical two- or three-year programs requiring advanced verbal or mathematical abilities. Even so much less diversity is offered in these programs than one might expect, given the professed commitment to local needs and student interests.

Community colleges too often use either the "cut and paste" method of program development or the "so many people want a course" method in developing occupational course offerings. In the cut and paste method, a school looks over several other two-year–college catalogs and selects the courses it will offer. This selection may or may not reflect the needs of the area. In the so many people want a course method, numbers rather than vocational needs dictate choice. Many colleges have excellent programs ideally designed to fit local needs and student abilities, but more such programs are needed (Johnson, 1969). In most states, too little emphasis has been given to them. At present a trend is developing toward greater emphasis on career education.

Another program area often found in the community college is continuing education. Continuing education is distinct from occupational education in that the courses are not designed to develop a particular vocational skill. The courses may increase the student's earning power as a side effect, but they are offered primarily to satisfy individual educational needs. Courses such as

painting, flower arranging, and powder-puff mechanics illustrate this category. Local interests largely dictate these offerings.

Sometimes community colleges offer a program of community services. The curriculum may include a variety of cultural, educational, or community service programs, such as lectures, movies, surveys, and consulting services. The exact nature of the activities varies according to the size and orientation of the particular college.

General education courses are also offered in many community colleges (and usually required of everyone). These courses are designed to develop basic educational goals such as citizenship, effective use of leisure time, and effective home management. Such goals are vague and considerable controversy arises over how they can best be met. General education courses are not specialized. They may include a variety of introductory courses in fields such as psychology, sociology, and government. College administrators assume that general-education objectives will be met somewhere in the process even though specific objectives are not stated.

The preceding summary suggests that two-year college leaders have fairly well defined the purposes and programs of their institutions. This is not the case. Educational leaders disagree even about the relative importance of transfer versus occupational programs (the two most widely accepted functions). We feel that general education must become the overriding mission of the two-year college. Establishing a separate category—general education— is self-defeating since one can then assume that it may be met separately. The development of an effective system of instruction should clarify this point. In fact, traditional programs of remedial education need not be a separate function either. They can (and should) be an integral part of the various programs.

Many community-college spokesmen feel that the seventies will be a crucial decade for the two-year college. Can it be all things to all people or has it already demonstrated that its collegiate identity prevents it from offering educational opportunities to all? Some educators insist upon a liberal education for everyone. They argue

that the search for critical standards, the patient construction of theory, the effort to distinguish between what is enduring and what is evanescent, and the pursuit of knowledge are ends in themselves (Hutchins, 1968, p. 121). Hutchins (p. 154) suggests that in view of the rapidity of change, specific vocational training can best be done by industry: "The special role of educational institutions would seem to be liberal, to be continuously open to those who use their minds in some systematic way or to lay the foundations for doing so."

Cohen (1969, p. 14) generally agrees that industry can train individuals in the vocational fields. He suggests, however, that training programs be cooperatively worked out with community-college personnel. Cohen also suggests that some form of "liberal, general education" is desirable for developing values in students. Cohen argues that the curriculum should lead "a learner to acquire a sense of social integration, an awareness of himself, and a sense of his place in the matrix of society. He is led to gain value structures on his own through learning of the values held by his contemporaries and historical predecessors and through viewing the culture milieu in which they live and have lived. . . . It must be an interdisciplinary institutional thrust, one that is built on principles of integration, and effect on individuals" (Cohen, 1969, p. 150).

Chase (1966, p. 298) echoes this sentiment arguing that the problem of developing a system of values is "perhaps [the] most crucial concern of education today." In his discussion of change in society and its effect on education, Chase (p. 292) states that education must develop a greater "openness to the world" in students if these students are to succeed. Michael (1966, p. 15) concurs: "The student must learn to learn, for he will need to grow intellectually during his entire lifetime in order to avoid obsolescence."

Students no longer accept teacher authority in deciding what they are to learn. Community-college students want course content to be relevant to contemporary society. "Now more than ever before our students are actively seeking for authenticity in their education, for real relevance, for genuine and dependable commitment" (Garrison, 1969, pp. 149–150).

14

Failure of Traditional Roles

Increasing attention must be given to defining educational goals which go beyond simple mastery of content (Goodlad, 1966, p. 11). Content should not be a series of blocks of information isolated from one another (content for content's sake) but a unified whole, contributing to the student's understanding of the world. Today, knowledge is expanding so rapidly that one cannot hope to keep up with all of it. This concept dislodges many cherished ideas concerning teaching and learning. It particularly upsets the instructor who thinks of himself as a dispenser of information. The knowledge explosion requires the instructor to select the information to be "dispensed," realizing even then that the learner must do most of the learning on his own.

Paradoxically the one constant element in our present society seems to be change—more accurately, extremely rapid change. We are hard pressed to predict what changes will occur in twenty years or even ten. What does this lack of predictability mean in terms of education? "In the new social structure we are developing and in the new cultural configuration that is emerging, the emphasis is on methodologies rather than metaphysics, on new symbolic systems for analysis and expression rather than dogmatic 'solutions,' and on the centrality of man acting in uncertainty. . . . Our emergent pattern of living calls for coping skills or competencies that may bear little resemblance to what we have been accustomed to acknowledge as the objectives of instruction in our schools" (Gow and others, 1966, pp. 198–199).

Course content in community colleges must also be considered in the light of increasing specialization. New disciplines develop as general fields become specialized. By overspecializing, an individual may become isolated from the larger question of how his efforts relate. "Indeed, modern man is a specialist, and specialization requires knowledge in depth of a particular discipline or profession. But such depth is a reform of existential dilettantism unless, standing in his specialty, the specialist sees his work as related to his life, his discipline as related to other disciplines, and his knowledge as related to the world of action and value" (Kolb, 1966, pp. 55–60).

In the future, the community college will go in many differ-

15

ent directions, depending upon community setting and needs. Its programs will undoubtedly become increasingly more complex, and specialization will become the rule. All students will need to be shown how to operate effectively in an increasingly complex society. Relevance of materials and programs will become essential in order to respond to the demand for increasing competence. The student will be treated more as an individual—an individual who will take charge of his own learning. Education will be a matter of life-long learning. Under such a system, the development of learning skills and the development of a viable personal value system will be of primary importance. Course content will help the individual understand his environment, so that he can effectively live and work in any given environment.

We will soon know how to arrange learning sequences effectively for almost any learner at any age. Will this knowledge get into the schools? Possessing knowledge and applying it are two different things. However, public educational institutions at all levels will soon be compelled to change and adapt to new techniques. If they do not, commercial educators who are ready to guarantee results will compete for the right to educate our citizens. In fact, this is already happening (*Education Turnkey News,* 1970). Taxpayers and legislators are demanding results.

The underlying assumption of our work is that most students can indeed master what we have to teach them—given sufficient time and appropriate instruction. Indeed, it is the obligation of the college to make students successful.

2

Failure of
Traditional Attitudes

Many two-year college students do not possess academic skills and abilities commensurate with those of students entering four-year colleges. We have labeled these students nontraditional. Statements of purpose typically recognize the nontraditional as well as the traditional students and reflect the need for a broad range of programs and services to meet the needs of all entering students. Unfortunately, however, statements of purpose are inert. *People* are responsible for the success or failure of any program. If staff orientation falls short of fully covering the stated goals, the final outcome will also fall short of these goals. If people do not implement programs as intended, the goals will not be achieved. The problem has two sides. First, the underlying philosophical base of most teaching and learning is too narrow to sustain the many goals of the community college and needs of the student. Second, the techniques or methods of instruction are much too general and vague and do not

17

permit a realistic approach to teaching or learning. We examine the first aspect of the problem in this chapter.

When we speak of the philosophical base of instruction we are referring to the way beliefs and attitudes have been traditionally ordered with respect to teaching and learning. We are suggesting that congruence of purpose and action cannot be achieved unless instructional attitudes cover *all* entering students. The following description illustrates how narrow the present philosophical base for teaching and learning is. Not all schools, fortunately, fit this extreme picture. However, a large number of them are quite accurately described, and a sizable number of community colleges are certainly included in the picture:

> [The] grading and course credit system is a reflection of our free enterprise economy. The faculty represents management; the student represents labor; and grades represent wages. . . . It is always the object of management to get a maximum expenditure of energy out of labor with a minimum of output of wages. . . . When the student has received his wages in the form of a passing grade, he then uses it to purchase his green stamp in the form of a course credit, and when he has accumulated the requisite number of these and his little book is full, he takes the book to the registrar and exchanges it for his diploma—which makes the registrar simply a clerk in a redemption center [Cole, 1966, pp. 46–47].

Yet, if the college sees itself as a sorter of pupils into various levels of achievement according to normative evaluation and treatment, it cannot really be oriented to the individual student. If teaching is viewed as the transmitting of subject matter to a given child, rather than as the development in a child of a given set of competencies, then it cannot be said that the teacher's foremost concern is the individual. It makes little difference how a teacher organizes subject matter or varies his teaching methods if his emphasis is primarily on the subject. It makes little sense to give teachers a highly effective teaching strategy if they are unable to demonstrate the soundness of a course in terms of its value to students.

Most general educational objectives are of necessity general statements of societal goals—that is, expressions of the society's expectations or perhaps its demands. They are not static goals but

18

are subject to modification as society changes. Success of the education system is measured in terms of its students' abilities to compete successfully in society. A lag exists between the changing expectations of society and school instruction. This lag is to be expected because it takes time for societal goals to be defined, to be accepted, and to become a functioning part of a school curriculum.

General educational goals (principles) are dynamic, rather than static entities. They are not eternal truths; rather, they are tentative working guidelines for educators to use when designing various curricular patterns. The tentative nature of so-called "principles" is the crux of the problem. How can educators best continually update their guidelines and reduce the implementation lag? Specifically, how can they make teaching and learning fit contemporary societal expectations? Are there values upon which a general philosophy of education might be based and which are broad enough to encompass the dynamic nature of the educational process? We try to answer these difficult questions later in this chapter.

First, however, we must consider another factor which has a pronounced effect on the operation of all social institutions. This factor may be defined as the sociopolitical orientations of the college staff and supporting bodies. Blocker and others (1965, p. 67) describe this factor as follows: "Individual perceptions of the two-year college are influenced by sociopolitical orientations. Consequently, the functions emphasized or ignored by a specific institution depend upon the social referents of those who are in a position to contribute to its development. Because institutions must always be certain that their image is acceptable to a majority of their constituents, certain patterns of control and organization will predictably develop where corresponding types of thought patterns prevail." Orientation patterns range from reactionary to radical. The conservative and the liberal positions are the most common.

A suggested rationale for teaching and learning follows rather closely the liberal orientation described by Blocker and others. Though the liberal pattern is considered dominant in American society, it is not dominant in two-year colleges. Whereas the reactionary and conservative positions emphasize individual responsibility and tradition, with the transmission of traditional culture

19

center stage, the liberal and radical positions are pragmatic, with education constantly adapting to serve as a primary agent of social change. (See Table 1.)

We argue that individual learning is central and that the responsibility for producing learning—behavioral change in the learner—lies with the teacher. Yet, the individual, rather than the institution, should determine the direction and degree of social change or reconstruction. The college should recognize the needs of society and provide the tools and cognitive skills for systematic problem-solving and reasoned value judgments. In this sense the institution works to bring about change without usurping the right of the students to determine their goals. It neither dictates to society what it should do nor sits back and waits for society to tell it what to do. The individual is central. However, present faculty orientations are not likely to support such a system. The college must become an interactive social institution. The philosophical base for teaching and learning depends upon such interaction. Community residents must interact with school personnel in order to establish general educational goals. Students and faculty must interact to establish specific learning objectives. Interaction should be continuous to assure that the dynamic nature of society is reflected in the curriculum. But interaction is futile if teachers honestly believe that some students are incapable of achieving. Many teachers think that some groups are unable to learn—blacks, poor whites, and Chicanos most notably. Teachers must be convinced that *all* students can learn—not just those who have previously demonstrated success. Curriculum programs should be viewed as serving different needs of the diverse student body and no status ranks should be placed on the programs. A one-year vocational program is just as necessary and important as a college transfer program. The sole distinction is that they serve different needs. The difficulty with traditional attitudes is that they often consider some courses or programs inherently more valuable and uplifting than others and perpetuate static values.

Basic Philosophical Model

We have presented the learner as the central figure in the educational process. Society, or the individual's environment, directs,

Table 1. SOCIOPOLITICAL POSITIONS

	Radical	Liberal	Conservative	Reactionary
Attitude Toward Change	Rapid Change	Gradual Change	Maintenance of Status Quo	Regression to The Past
Attitude Toward Government Organization	Highly Centralized	Centralized for Special Services for Selected Groups	Decentralized for Essential Services for Selected Groups	Laissez-faire
Implications for Education	Educational Programs for Social Reconstruction	Educational Programs for Gradual Change	Educational Programs for Preservation of Culture	Educational Programs for Preservation of Absolute Values
	Directed Curriculum for Social Objectives	Curriculum Adapted to Current Problems and Needs	Curriculum Centered upon Traditional Subject Matter	Curriculum Limited to Immutable Truths
	Selection of Students for Social Purposes	Self-Selection of Students	Selection of Students on Academic Basis	Selection of Students on Academic, Social, and Economic Basis

Source: Clyde E. Blocker, Robert H. Plummer, and Richard C. Richardson, Jr., *The Two-Year College: A Social Synthesis,* © 1965. By permission of Prentice-Hall, Inc.

limits, or expands his alternatives and generally prescribes the acceptable boundaries of his actions. Any philosophy of education must deal with the problem of teaching the student how best to interact with his environment. Other teaching efforts must be considered supportive. Perhaps the most damning theme of educational critics is that the educational process extinguishes the natural curiosity of children and soon makes learning a tedious and bothersome procedure. Leonard (1968) insists that education should be made ecstatic. Learning should be fun and interesting. Granted, not all that one must learn is fun; however, the student should at least view his material as relevant in and necessary for dealing with his environment. The present goals of education were intended to provide this relevance. Their fault lies in the assumption that all learners wish to deal with the same environment in the same ways, to the same degree, and for the same reasons. We think not. Educators must explore ways for individuals to find acceptable alternatives which fulfill social expectations *and* individual psychological needs. Education ought to capitalize on man's natural desire to be rational and to understand his environment and his place in it. Today, youth wants answers, not platitudes or stock answers based on memorized moralities. They want you to "tell it like it is." And they want you to help them find out how they fit in or whether they fit in.

The type of philosophical base we are suggesting must view the teaching-learning process as open. That is, one which is flexible enough to incorporate the needs of society and at the same time recognize and foster the needs of individual students. Further, the philosophical base must be consistent with a society in which the rapidity of change is almost overwhelming. Teaching students how to learn on their own must replace the practice of presenting set bodies of content at fixed rates.

Mooney (1954) suggests an instructional model which fits our criteria. Mooney describes a four-step sequence: openness (perception)—O, integration (holding information)—I, transaction (using information)—T, and creation (successful application)—C. The Mooney model is especially compelling because it is flexible and particularly suited to a dynamic society. Mooney views every in-

22

stitution as an independently interacting social entity. According to such a construct, education is one type of institution composed of a series of interactive social processes. Ultimate individual behavior is determined by the combined experiences the individual has in all the socially interactive institutions to which he is exposed. Theoretically, the result of the experiences is an independent individual —an individual increasingly able to control his destiny.

Mooney (1954) further contends that "we know what we are living *against* but not what we are living *for*." In terms of education, we usually know what a student may *not* do, but it is likely that we have not decided exactly what we *will* let him do. We are equipped for reaction but not for action. This procedure seems to uphold the contention that education operates according to a conservative sociopolitical pattern. Institutions ought to anticipate problems so that they are not forced into reactive modes of behavior.

Mooney suggests that we need a positive concept of the individual in the learning process. "Creation" is the key factor in his OITC system. Mooney uses the term in its literal sense rather than the various normative definitions in "creativity" literature. An individual must be judged against what he does, not what a group has done before. A premium is put on what one does or produces after experiencing a learning situation. The outcomes of a learning sequence are to be judged on an individual basis—not against group performance levels. This criterion is hard to apply because most of what is written about creativity uses some group measure. For example, if you were to invent a better mousetrap, it would have to be unique or at least substantially different from existing models in order to be considered creative by society. But if you had never seen a mousetrap and invented the common everyday mousetrap, your work would be considered creative by Mooney's standards. Such a product would be considered creative if it were new or unique to the producer, even though it were historically "old."

Learning is a process of continually improving one's sense perceptions and handling the information obtained in increasingly complex and powerful ways. The beauty of this model is that it places the learner at the center of all learning, transforms the evaluation of learning. The individual is constantly satisfying environmental needs rather than meeting arbitrary group requirements. In the Mooney model, learning is justified in terms of the effectiveness of the learner's "creations" (solutions) in understanding his environment.

Mooney's model is founded on the assumption that the growth patterns of all organisms are similar. Although man is the most developed of all organisms, he too must stand or fall with his environment, depending upon how well he understands and adapts. As suggested earlier, he must be made aware of his environment and its problems (societal needs) and then be given the skills to deal with them effectively. We believe that Mooney's approach should serve as a model for community-college administrators. The sole aim of education is to permit the individual to understand and to interact with his environment fully; that is, to move the individual as far as possible into increasingly complex and powerful operations (solutions of his problems). Administrators must be careful not to lose sight of this purpose. There is a danger that the college—rather than the purpose of that institution—may become an end in itself.

Schools, then, should work for the most complete development of each individual possible, and the teacher should function as a manager of learning, not as a dispenser of information. However, as an institution becomes complex, a series of worker roles evolve: administrative roles, counselor roles, budget officer roles, teacher roles, and so on. Sometimes these roles conflict with the most important role—the learner role.

The key to individualization of instruction is positive reinforcement of successful learning experiences and appropriate practice throughout the learning sequences. It may be trite to say that one does not learn to be a carpenter without building something, but teachers nonetheless lose sight of this essential idea. One does not teach a person to be a "responsible citizen" if, as a student, he is never given responsibilities. One does not teach the principles of democracy if the entire school structure is highly authoritarian. Consider this example: The dean of students of a community college believed that the dress code needed to be revised to be in line with

24

current fashions. (Miniskirts, culottes, scooter skirts, and so forth were constant sources of dispute and confusion.) The dean checked with the faculty and concluded that the matter could best be settled by the students themselves in their senate. A special committee of students active in the senate was subsequently formed. These young people gave the project much time and effort and finally arrived at a viable and consistent policy which was more liberal than the existing code but was far from being a reversal of it. The students presented their proposals to the dean, who passed them on to the administrative council. In the meantime, however, many parents became concerned that the students were "running the school." Some teachers were approached by parents. Teachers who had been outraged over the promiscuous nature of miniskirts and the like were encouraged and suddenly became vocal in and out of school. As a result, the student policy was soundly castigated by most of the faculty and ignored by the administrative council. Regardless of one's views on "excessive exposure," the students had been unfairly treated. They had been told to create a product and had been led to believe that their efforts, if done honestly and reasonably, would be accepted. How much credibility do you suppose the faculty and administration at this college will have the next time the students there are asked to "create" something?

It may also be trite to say that one needs lumber to build his house. Yet this idea is also frequently ignored. A student assigned a term paper on the New Deal may fail if he finds few references in the school library; more likely, he will not know how to use the library or to organize an abundance of information. The teacher must see that resources are available *and* that the learner is capable of using them.

The learner must have the freedom to make decisions about his work, and he needs to have his work "rewarded." Picture a teacher walking into a class and saying, "We have just finished the unit on Latin American culture and we are ready to start another unit. What do you want to study next?" Someone says, "Let's talk about Latin American agricultural products." "That's an interesting topic," the teacher responds. "Where do bananas come from?"

Another student says, "I think they are shipped to the United States." The teacher then says, "Does anyone know how the bananas go from the plantations to the ships? Remember, we learned how poor the countries were and said that the geography made transportation difficult." At this point the class is silent. They know they have been "had." The teacher is going to talk about transportation problems of Latin America and intended to do so *all along*. This example may appear extreme, but is it really? Have you ever been told you "could do what you wanted to" only to discover that, for one reason or another, only limited alternatives were considered "reasonable"?

Mooney's system is individualistic, yet seems remarkably adaptable to psychologists' models of human thought processes. The system is meaningful to those who stress the role of education in fostering the development of individual value systems, to those concerned with behavioral outcomes, and to those, such as Bruner and Bloom, who develop practical systems to tie learning theory to classroom teaching.

Teacher Roles

The teacher knows or is expected to know how the elements of his field fit together and relate to the general environment. His experience should enable him to teach in a way that allows his students to gain insight into their environment. The teacher also should know how to help students learn how to learn in his subject area. Many teachers get lost in their content. They seem to forget why they are teaching a subject. The teacher should not view his subject matter as static but rather as constantly subject to revision as new information or insights suggest. He must communicate his knowledge and at the same time be sensitive to how his students are receiving his information. The teacher cannot produce openness unless the process itself is open. Therefore, the teacher must operate in a give-and-take atmosphere. He must encourage each student to develop his own understanding of the subject so that it more closely approximates the teacher's. (We assume that the teacher has insight and viewpoints worthy of teaching—he has some truths, if not facts. This truth may be the ability to discern bias in the written word.) The teacher must first find out where the students are in order to provide a base for subsequent communication. He must then establish a sequential give-and-take communications system. Mooney (1966, p. 9) suggests he ask himself: Is the communication vital? Do I come to life in my expression? Have I heard the student? Do I watch and listen for clues for later communications? Do I have an objective for the student? Am I open to different minds? Am I testing what areas are open and what areas are closed in my students' minds? Do I know what blocks various students have to effective expression?

In short, the teacher must be constantly alert to errors in the communication process, looking for sender and receiver errors and striving for simultaneous translation. When this point is reached, both parties become equal operators; each draws from and adds to the other's understanding. The system becomes open, and the teaching-learning process becomes charged and alive. This system is the converse of the traditional teacher-to-learner communication system, in which the only stimulus is the teacher's voice—probably perceived by students as annoying static.

Integration, the next phase of our teaching model, encompasses more than the teacher's actions. According to Mooney, "through the teacher as its agent, the culture of a given time passes on what men in that field *then* think to be important" (1966, p. 11, emphasis added). This stage might be called determining the relevance of knowledge. The idea of relevance is consistent with the liberal sociopolitical pattern of thought, which holds that learning is a process of continual correction of information and that the outcome of the education process should be greater unity of knowledge. The whole is greater than the sum of its parts. For example, a person takes several separate courses, each with certain major objectives and each explaining some part of the individual's environment. By trying to integrate his new knowledge into previous knowledge, the individual may derive generalizations about his environment which were not specifically taught in any *one* course. Any educational practices which cannot be clearly related to increased environmental understanding should be eliminated from the system.

How can an individual teacher assist his students to understand and operate in their environment? Such a question is concerned primarily with the why of knowledge rather than the what of knowledge. All human efforts past and present are viewed as part of an evolutionary process. What man has done and is doing is not the central issue but is instead the raw material from which meanings are derived. Students should be taught to consider the why of man's past and present actions and to evaluate such actions in terms of their effectiveness in advancing or retarding man's future development. The teacher might ask himself whether he knows the key questions for his area. Does he ask *why* questions? Is the student given time to develop connections? Is the course organized in a way which develops such questions?

If the first two stages (openness and integration) have been developed, the student should be able to transform his information into problem solutions or even into unique solutions. But, he must be given the freedom to attempt these solutions, encouraged to try out new ideas, and shown by example that alternatives usually exist. Recognizing the need for alternatives in the learning process is particularly important. The teacher might ask questions or present problems for which there are no best or right answers. He might encourage individual students to do independent work. He cannot assess a particular student's performance using group standards. Creative solutions cannot be put on a numerical scale. The notion of transformation of information to produce problem solutions is based on flexibility of individual action. The standard should be the effectiveness of the transformation, not lock-step adherence to prescribed rules. The teacher's job should be to assist the individual in developing effective methods for holding and using his knowledge. But these methods must not be thought of as rigid. A closed system tends to retard learning and decrease individual independence. Sociologists tell us that society is becoming more and more closed. Educators in all social institutions, especially in the community colleges, should be leaders in increasing man's potential.

Some Other Views

Dale (1966, p. 108) says that the purpose of education and the "goal of all learning is to develop the independent learner— the mature individual who no longer needs the protective counsel and guidance of the school or college. . . . The aim is to decrease dependent learning and increase independent learning." Cohen (1969, p. 37) says: "The true end of all instruction is to help all students learn how to think." Hutchins (1968) says that education should be "the deliberate, organized attempt to help people to become intelligent . . . [and that education should be] interested in the development of human beings . . . its aim is not manpower, but manhood." Education is also defined (Thelen, 1961) as the "process of participating in inquiry under such conditions that one learns to inquire more effectively." Shumsky (1965) feels that "the greatest challenge for education is to make knowledge a part of the lives of students and to make subject matter personally meaningful." Shumsky discusses teacher styles exhaustively and concludes that traditional schemes put learners into a passive mold, or, as he says "(1965, p. 17) an object to be moved, rather than as a subject that has the potential to fly." Burton (1962, p. 55) describes the ideal learning situation as one in which "a pupil is placed in a situation where *he* needs to know or to acquire some skill *he* needs and *sees* that he needs." Bruner (1966, p. 1) defines instruction as "an effort to assist or shape growth." He further contends (p. 35) that the curriculum "should involve the mastery of skills that in turn lead to the mastery of still more powerful ones, the establishment of self-reward sequences." Tyler (1966, p. 20) reviews the state of research in learning and concludes that "the picture of the human individual which is now emerging is one of a dynamic organism, acting in ways which will help him attain his values as well as seeking to meet his basic biological needs." He adds further that much of the behavior formerly thought to be some type of stimulus and response activity may be explained "as an active effort on his part (that is,

29

the individual) to manipulate his environment to attain his values" (p. 200).

Most modern educators agree that the individual is the key to the entire system of formal education. Most teachers agree also. Yet, herein lies the paradox. Although teachers agree they are likely to point out the need for order or control of their class groups. One cannot have a highly individualistic mode of education which is incompatible with and at the same time have various means of administrative orderings which are designed primarily to facilitate teacher or administrative control of groups. The only controls that are justifiable are those which can demonstrably be tied to the learning efficiency of individual students.

Bruner (1966, p. 127) says: "The will to learn is an intrinsic motive, one that finds both its source and its reward in its own extrinsic exercise. The will to learn becomes a 'problem' only under specialized circumstances like those of a school, where a curriculum is set, students confined, and a path fixed." All that we have said above can be summed up in one sentence: How can education be made individualistic so that it becomes an intrinsic need of its students?

Although community colleges have a unique mission, traditional methods of teaching will not enable these colleges to meet individual needs. The traditional philosophy of education is too narrow. Educational goals are best pictured as dynamic guidelines for assisting educators in developing relevant educational programs rather than as static "educational principles." The liberal outlook is predominant in our rapidly changing society as a whole, but not among educators. A general philosophy broad enough to encompass dynamic educational goals centers on the student and his environment and pictures the two components as interactive. This philosophy views the end product of student learning as the unique solutions to problems which collectively expand and deepen student understanding of his world and enable him to become an active participant in his environment. Such a philosophy requires a method or vehicle through which educators can make individualized instruction a reality.

3

New Learning Principles

Two major psychological schools of thought regarding learning may be identified: the cognitive field theory and the stimulus-response theory. Each school contains a variety of sub-theories, and individual theorists are often far from agreeing with others in their own camp. To further the confusion, a third major school is developing. Theorists in this group are attempting to reconcile the ideas of the other two schools so that a single, unified learning theory may be developed. Theorists in the third school have studied the major aspects of cognitive field theory and stimulus-response theory and believe that they have found common elements. Some of these integrationists contend that terminology is a major source of confusion and that rival theories may (if terms were clarified) be advocating parallel ideas. A brief nontechnical description of the two major learning-theory positions follows. Readers who wish detailed and technical treatment are referred to Hilgard's *Theories of Learning* (1966), which is considered by many the major work

31

in this area. Cohen (1969, pp. 181–182) summarizes the two major positions as follows:

> Cognitive theory includes elements of dynamism, general organizational patterns, and gestalt theory. Stimulus-response theory is that which is usually associated with classical and operant conditioning, rote learning, and associationism. Cognitive theory recognizes elements of general consciousness, insight, and intuitiveness which cannot be explained by known connections among learned events, whereas stimulus-response theory views the mind as changing in reaction to connections built up through series of trials and associations.

We believe that an eclectic theory is necessary and that both affective (attitudinal elements) and cognitive elements must be combined in an interactive theory. (The interactive theory closely parallels the integrationist theory discussed above. However, the interactive theory places more emphasis on attitude development and positive self-concepts.) This position is mandatory given the philosophical base developed in the preceding chapter.

Learning Theory

Bruner (1966, p. 7) suggests that the following features constitute the minimum framework of a learning theory: predispositions toward learning, a structure about which the materials or ideas are organized, the sequence in which the materials or ideas are presented, and the nature of rewards and punishments. A. Cohen (1969, p. 85) uses essentially the same factors but amplifies the first to "environment or set of experiences which implant a predisposition to learn." He also uses "the most effective mode of presentation" as his third component.

Structure refers to the hierarchical ordering of material. Shumsky (1965, p. 75) says that the "teacher initiates the structures for systematic, serious study which have built into them continued teacher-pupil planning of subsequent structures." We subscribe to this viewpoint. The teacher is expected to be the subject-matter expert capable of separating the important from the trivial, the relevant from the irrelevant, and the interesting from the dull. On him rests the major responsibility for planning the course. However, if the teacher is to fit our model, he must never lose sight of the central importance of the learner. He must always encourage full learner participation in planning.

Bruner (1966, pp. 44–48) sets forth three considerations for developing a learning structure: mode of representation, economy of information (or the amount of information that must be held in mind and processed to achieve comprehension), and the power of the information (the capacity to associate matters that, on the surface, seem quite separate). Bruner (1966, p. 11) identifies three modes or bases of learning: the enactive mode (including activities such as swimming and walking), the iconic mode (including visual or other sensory organization and summary imagery), and the symbolic mode (including language and abstract manipulations). Each of these modes is more powerful than the one before it, and each represents a necessary part of individual intellectual growth. Many community-college students are not adept in the symbolic mode. Many (perhaps most) students have impoverished imagerial systems (incomplete or faulty models of the world). Before the teacher can hope to bring about significant learning, he must raise the student's level of abstraction. However, a raising of the level of abstraction cannot be done until or unless the student has built effective storage models. Therefore a variety of media must be used in instruction—alternatives must be made available to suit many learner styles.

The following example may illustrate. Imagine a teacher trying to teach the concept of latitude and longitude to a group of learners with low abstraction ability without an image for them to manipulate. He would not get far. Now imagine him using an orange as a model. If he has the students peel the orange, separate the sections, and lay them out horizontally, almost all the principles of latitude and longitude, including distortion at the poles, become easily observable. In subsequent discussions with the same learners, they can refer to the orange.

The structure of a course can include a wide variety of learning activities to accommodate different learning styles. Glaser

33

(1966) suggests that the teacher should decide how the learner can best master the subject matter. He also recognizes that varying types of presentations are required. Gagne (1970, p. 41) extends the notion that various objectives call for different types of behavior: "There seem to be classes of behavior, the members of which have a formal identity irrespective of their particular content. These classes of behavior can be described as performances (that is, as objectives) and distinguished from each other." This statement adds a final element to the concept of structure, namely, that one can identify in a hierarchical manner sets of behaviors and performances.

In summary, structure is a complex problem requiring careful analyses of the content presented and the performance expected. The selection of content and behavioral operations will determine how the subject matter may best be presented and ordered for individual learners. Also, the abilities of individual learners will limit the choices of subject matter.

The next component of our learning theory—sequence—is closely related to structure. Although in practice the two probably cannot be divided, they are separated here to help clarify our analysis. Sequence concerns the *way* one elects to divide an instructional block or unit to best facilitate individual learning. Shaping behavior can be thought of as the way an instructional sequence is broken into short steps. Each step begins with input (information we feel the learner needs), then allows for practice (a chance to see whether the learner can do something with the input), and ends with feedback (to let the learner know whether he is proceeding correctly). As many practice cycles as necessary are given until the learner has reached the objective. Bruner (1966, pp. 49–50) defines instruction as "leading [the] learner through a sequence of statements and restatements of a problem or body of knowledge that increase the learner's ability to grasp, transform, and transfer what he is learning." He argues against rigidified sequences. An ideal sequence, he says, cannot be specified independent of the learner.

Feigenbaum (1963, p. 299) feels that "there are certain elementary information processes which an individual must perform

34

if he is to discriminate, memorize, and associate verbal items, and that these information processes participate in all the cognitive activity of all individuals." Although Feigenbaum is describing the rote memorization processes, the assertion that particular processes operate in all cognitive activity for all individuals is profound. If this theory proves true for all levels of thought, then the teacher need only design materials according to the sequence of these processes and let each student work at his own rate. This theory is one of the major underlying elements of commercial programing. Some general considerations apply to all students—assuming they are allowed to progress at varying rates and use a variety of materials. Carroll (1963, pp. 723–733) defines quality of instruction in terms of the degree to which presentation, explanation, and ordering of elements are individualized. The learner must be shown how to use his intellectual resources effectively. If the teacher considers the growth of thinking primary to all subjects, he must consider the following. Bruner (1966, p. 27) suggests that mental growth is not continuous but is like a staircase—a series of spurts and rests. This model suggests a series of prerequisites for each spurt. The teacher may first have to improve his student's ability to associate and discriminate items of information before he can expect him to manipulate entire concepts. Real progress begins as the student begins to grasp and manipulate simple concepts. These, in turn, enable him to build complex chains of concepts (principles and strategies). The community-college student often needs a greater degree of concrete visual imagery than his university counterpart who has well developed abilities of abstraction. Once the learner has developed a working image, he can be expected to operate in the same manner as any other learner. He is able to use his images to solve additional problems.

Problem-solving is viewed by computer-simulation psychologists as the combining of a series of suboperations (plans). They contend that the way to improve the effectiveness of problem-solving is to improve subplans—for example, learning how to discriminate information and how to develop effective storage plans. The process might be compared to a person who is looking for an improperly filed letter and who gives up after a prolonged and fruitless search. The human mind is a vast storehouse of information. If information is poorly associated, it may become temporarily lost. Lost information may prevent problem solution. In addition to effective storage, one needs to develop cues so that one may call back information once stored. We might liken these cues to an index system. Problem-solving is a series of relatively simple mental operations. Careful sequencing of information can develop high degrees of problem-solving in all learners.

Simon (1959) contends that no qualitative difference may exist between creative and less creative individuals as far as their thought processes are concerned. He argues that creative individuals develop new conceptual models from inconsistencies they perceive in existing models, while less creative individuals are content to use the existing ones. However, both develop the means to work with these models in essentially the same way. The teacher must encourage an open, flexible, and questioning atmosphere which fosters the development of new models.

The last element in our learning theory is reward and punishment. To be effective, rewards and punishments must become self-generating rather than being externally imposed. The learner should derive his own reward from successful accomplishment. If external grading is used, it should be on an individual basis. An individual graded against a group—especially a group he is unable to compete with—knows before he starts that he will gain little reward. If we are to depend on self-generating rewards, we must enable the learner to achieve success in his own right. We must convince the learner that his goal is to accomplish clearly defined objectives at his own rate, not to compete against a group. Once we have done this, we have begun to apply positive reinforcement and to establish an internal reward system. Success develops the desire for more success.

The present reward systems tend to establish two groups of students: the approved and the disapproved. The students who can most readily adapt to the system gain approval. Those students who have the most difficulty adapting to the system get little or no approval. Shumsky (1965, p. 76) feels that a pattern is established early in the student's education and that the pattern becomes increasingly more pronounced, leading to the eventual dropout of many students in the disapproved group. Present evaluation criteria based upon group standards are responsible for this segregation. No reward is given, especially to the disapproved group. This problem reflects the most unfortunate aspects of Bloom's self-fulfilling prophecy—that teacher expectation fixes levels of student achievement.

The student operating under a self-reward system knows that his achievement will be measured against his capabilities. He knows that the amount of progress he makes from a fixed starting point will not be judged by group standards. Consequently, he is judged successful even though he takes longer to succeed than his classmates. The standards are not lowered; time is extended. The present norm-based grading systems do not operate in this manner. Instead, they relegate the slower members of a group to the bottom of the grade distribution for that group regardless of whether the student has shown progress and regardless of the amount of such progress. (In other words, the traditional grading system is not sensitive enough to show student progress when this progress is below a certain level—an F is an F even if it reflects much effort and progress.) In effect, the slow learner in such situations knows only that he cannot meet the standards. If our individualized system of teaching is to be effectively implemented, norm-referenced evaluation must be abandoned and replaced with individual performance goals as stated by behavioral objectives. (Chapter Six considers behavioral objectives in detail and suggests how they should be constructed and used.) This system makes common sense. Most people are much harder on themselves than they are on others. Suppose you try playing a game of golf by yourself. Although you have no opponent, you usually feel you could have done better no matter how well you score. Now suppose you are a twenty-two handicapper and that you play against a two handicapper without considering handicaps in the final score. You play out the round, but since there is no chance to win, you have little interest in the outcome.

These four components seem to present two focal points for

further discussion. The first and last components are centered on the attitudes of the individual: how he perceives beginning learning and how he forms impressions in a learning sequence (evaluative feedback). The other two components focus on systematic planning before and during instruction. Under this scheme, the teacher cannot be viewed simply as a dispenser of information. In such a role, he would be ignoring predispositions and rewards. Lee (1966, pp. 21–23) suggests that the teacher's role has changed and become specialized, concentrating on intellectualization and equipping a person so that he may learn over his entire lifetime.

This idea is consistent with our position on teaching and learning. We view the teacher as a manager of learning. In addition to having a basic knowledge of his subject, he must also become a specialist in designing instructional materials which allow individuals to progress at their own rates. In this sense the teacher's job orientation is singular rather than pluralistic. Self-instruction replaces group (pluralistic) teaching. The primary role of the teacher is to encourage and facilitate independent study. The teacher is not all things to all people. He is concerned with improving the ability of each student to master a set of learning objectives and to progress as far as he is able. The school cannot replace the home, the church, social welfare services, and so on, but it can assist students to realize their intellectual potential and build self-confidence through rewarding performance in learning. If clear objectives are presented and instructional sequences carefully designed to allow practice and feedback, the student knows where he is going and how he is doing throughout the learning sequence. If the sequence is then divided into short steps, each leading logically to the next step, the chance of a learner's successfully achieving the objectives is greatly increased. Under such a system the learner is constantly reenforced. Success breeds the desire for further success.

Many schools overemphasize the nonintellectual aspects of their curriculum, particularly for slower students. Often this group is believed unable to handle abstract material. Content is watered down and custodial holding actions result. We are not saying that traditional academically rigorous programs are the answer. Instead we agree with Bruner (1960, p. 33), who contends that any concept can be taught in some intellectually honest way to any student.

We have said that the role of the teacher has moved from the diversified to the specialized. In our context, this shift has two major implications. First, the teacher must become a specialist in learning. Second, the teacher must become aware of the relevance of his subject matter to his environment. These two important ideas are not stressed in most teacher preparation programs. Trainees are typically required to study educational-psychology courses which examine conflicting learning theories. They are usually expected to develop their own working set of learning principles. This approach may be valid if there is a central point around which such working principles may be constructed. Our central point is the individual. Such a focus provides the trainee with practical goals against which principles of learning may be evaluated.

Course requirements in the major field of the prospective teacher are often established without considering the pattern of the courses. Prospective teachers finishing an undergraduate degree often complain, "I just don't know enough to teach!" They are really saying that they do not know how the many courses they have taken fit together and relate to the contemporary needs of their students. It is easy to become lost in a specialty. The teacher constantly needs to strive for integration in his own thinking as he proceeds through his training. Such integration is especially critical for teachers if they are to pass it on to their students.

In order that each learner may operate according to his optimal learning pattern flexibility and planning must be improved. First, a variety of programs must be offered in order to accommodate a wide variety of individual learner styles. Second, differential learning rates must be built into the system. Finally, instruction and the evaluation of instruction must be based on individual achievement.

Behavior Change Process

What is learning? A. Cohen (1969, p. 7) presents the most cogent definition. Learning is "the changed capacity for, or tendency toward, acting in particular ways." Teaching or instruction, according to Cohen (p. 174), is the "application of treatments in a sequence designed to move people from one set of tendencies or competencies to another." And failure according to Cohen (p. 193) is the inability of the student "to cope with the mechanics of education." The key word in this last definition is mechanics. Cohen implies that failure is the result of the vagueness of instructional goals rather than weakness of student ability. In this sense, the school and the teacher, rather than the individual, fail. Hutchins (1968, p. 29) discusses the same problem, referring to it as educational shock. He says: "Those who have passed with the least shock into the system go farthest in it, [and] those to whom the shock is severe are labeled stupid and tolerated no longer than the law requires." Hutchins implies that learning cannot occur if the student is confounded and retarded by the system. This problem is particularly felt in the community college, which draws much of its student body from environments which make the student particularly susceptible to educational shock.

We have noted the four basic components of a learning theory: predispositions for learning; structure; sequence; and reward. Mink has developed a behavior change model which includes these four components and is consistent with the individualized procedures elaborated later in this book. The Mink model is based on the principle of reenforcement learning. In nontechnical terms this means that the instructor waits for a response and then takes appropriate action to develop a desired behavior. In the Mink model, the initial presentation is not a stimulus designed to evoke a given response. This procedure appears reasonable to us because it allows the teacher or counselor to concentrate on an observed behavior rather than trying to produce a behavior by manipulating the initial stimulus. Traditionally the teacher has tried to "motivate" a class for a given lesson or point he wishes to make. Trying to discover what will motivate a learner or group of learners is problematic, however. Teachers may spend considerable time motivating their students with little response. Real motivation comes from positive reenforcement of an unsolicited response, not from a series of abstract statements designed to make people want to do something. Under the reenforcement-learning process the teacher begins a lesson or presents a self-instructional unit and observes the responses of the class or collects information from individuals working through the unit. He then applies reenforcement principles to direct behavior. For maximum effect instruction should be individualized so that each student's behavior can be appropriately shaped or directed.

Learning in its natural state proceeds from a response. A small child hears sounds, makes a noise (response), and is reenforced. If he is rewarded he makes more sounds. If he is punished, he is less likely to make further sounds. If he is ignored he also begins to become more quiet. In short, a person does something and is then directed by the feedback from his action. A person can be told not to put his hand on hot coals, but real learning occurs when he touches those coals and gets burned. His response has been punished, and he will not readily make a similar response.

Steps in Behavior Change

Each step will be presented and then a brief discussion will follow suggesting how a given step might actually be applied in a school setting.

Step One: Identify the behavior to be encouraged and the behavior to be eliminated; then hold a conference with the student. Once defined, the desirable behavior can be developed and serve as a reference point against which possible undesirable behaviors can be identified. Personnel can then be expected to reward or reenforce desired behaviors and ignore undesirable behaviors.

Step Two: Obtain suggestions from the student about ways to change his behavior; explain objections to his behavior; offer suggestions; consult with other institutional personnel. The person making suggestions should be sure that the suggestions are consistent with the behavioral objectives defined by the total staff. Contradictions weaken the new desired behaviors, increase the time needed for the student to learn them, or cause the undesirable behavior to reoccur. If needed services or assistance are not available within the institution, the counseling staff should consult with outside agencies or refer the individual to the appropriate outside agency for help (reenforcement).

Step Three: Identify reenforcers of the undesirable behavior and determine who or what is providing the reenforcement. This step has traditionally been the province of the guidance and counseling staff. Extensive background information is typically collected from each student. We suggest limiting data collection to those items believed to have general implications for all students. Such data should be kept on file where they are readily available. Additional information about a specific student should be gathered as necessary for evaluating the causes of undesirable behaviors. Such information should be collected during student conferences. This system reduces initial data-collection time and frees counselors for one-to-one conferences. Para-professionals can be used for the routine initial data collection. The additional time required of teachers might be offset by the reduced amount of general information they would be expected to collect. The time spent in the above manner would have a closer relation to student progress than do student interest inventories or personality-assessment inventories, which typically must be extensively processed before they can be used for specific problem solution or behavior modification. These first three steps correspond to the predispositions phase of our learning theory.

Step Four: Decide upon a reenforcement that strengthens the new behavior and withhold reenforcement to eliminate undesirable behavior. The counselor or teacher should decide what actions to take to reenforce responses. Outside consultants may be brought in to suggest techniques and materials to assist the teacher. In-service workshops may be initiated to assist personnel in using the principles of reenforcement learning. This step corresponds to the structure component of a learning theory.

Step Five: Shape the new behavior. In this step counseling and teaching as distinct activities merge.

The five steps outlined above correspond to the systems approach to instruction, which is discussed in Chapter Four. Counselors may find themselves in the position of teachers—designing self-instructional products to reenforce desired behaviors. Teachers may find themselves in the position of counselors—designing affective as well as cognitive materials or learning activities. The administrator or specific learning activity may vary, but not the process. Step Five corresponds to the sequencing component of a learning theory. The teacher decides how to divide a learning sequence in order to provide maximum positive reenforcement. Both processes are designed to inform the learner clearly what he is to do and to provide constant practice and feedback so that he experiences a series of small successes (shaping behavior) which lead him to the desired end performance.

Steps One through Four provide the base for selecting the teaching objectives or behaviors to be shaped. Step Five is the application of counseling procedures within a sequence (course). If teachers individualize their courses according to the above steps, many undesirable behaviors cease. Much so-called undesirable or disruptive behavior is due to boredom, confusion, and constant negative reenforcement in the form of poor grades.

Step Six: Maintain the new behavior by using positive reenforcement, moving from a continuous reenforcement schedule to an occasional reenforcement schedule. This step is the continuation of the preceding one. Initially, the steps used in changing behavior are small and reenforcement is applied for each response. As the course progresses only completely correct responses or complete mastery of instructional objectives are rewarded. Finally, correct responses are only occasionally reenforced. Review material is periodically included in the newer learning units to provide occasional reenforcement and maintenance of desired behaviors.

Step Seven: Reshape behavior if the old undesirable behavior recurs and reexamine past actions. The instructor should collect information about the success of his materials. Revision data sheets and error-rate studies tell him what sections of his materials were clear, weak, poor, or irrelevant. Based on such information from the learners the materials are revised. Steps Six and Seven are roughly comparable to the reward-and-punishment component of a learning theory. Thus, our behavior-change model incorporates elements from all four components of a learning theory.

In summary, a teaching rationale for the community college must provide a means for changing behaviors. The teacher and the student must keep in mind carefully stated objectives describing the desired behavioral outcomes expected of each learner. These objectives are the key to translating a general philosophical learning theory into a practical, workable rationale for the teacher on the job.

Such a rationale requires systematic planning. The community college is, because of its multiple purposes, a highly complex institution. Haphazard organization or instruction cannot be tolerated. The entire operation must be united around the primary responsibility of the institution—causing student learning. Admittedly, learning, as it has been considered here, is a complex phenomenon. We have noted, however, that sound principles of learning exist which can be systematically employed to reduce the element of chance in the learning process. Industry, recognizing the need to reduce haphazard learning, has for years used a systems approach in solving complex problems. United States space efforts provide a dramatic illustration of the power of such an approach.

New Instructional Principles

*W*e have argued in the preceding chapters that learning should be a systematic process which allows for individual learning rates and is directed toward enlarging the learner's store of relevant concepts, thereby increasing the effectiveness of his thinking. Improving student learning requires clearly stated goals at all levels— institutional, departmental, and for individual courses. These goals must be stated in terms of measurable student behavior change. Improving student learning also requires a systematic organization of the teaching-learning process which fosters individual learning rates.

Objectives and Goals

In this chapter we use the terms *goals* and *objectives*. We define a goal as the final end of something, for instance of a program or a course. An objective is a specific end which one must accomplish in order to reach a final end. In practice, both terms

should be stated as measurable elements. Clearly stated goals and objectives provide administrative personnel, teachers, and learners with direction and perspective. They provide a basis for evaluation and reduce uncertainty. They also provide a basis for program evaluation at the administrative level and articulation with the community and other social institutions.

We may be unable to assess the results of our goals except over a long period. We may be aiming at student participation in the next election. But unless the student is of voting age, we must wait to assess results. We may hope that a learner will keep at a task until he has mastered it with no mistakes; but evaluation may have to be delayed. The delay may require a later follow-up or open-ended time periods beyond normal course blocks. If we state goals and objectives in concrete behavioral terms, we have to increase flexibility in our grading and scheduling procedures. The alternative is to select only low-level goals and objectives which we are certain the student will accomplish within an established time period.

We have previously discussed predisposition to learning, structure, sequence, and man's need to understand and control his environment. How does he do all this? He strives for goals. The overriding goal of education is the modification of behavior to make the learner more independent and self-sustaining in his environment.

Lombard (1965, p. 33) suggests that "since we are far more likely to realize those objectives that we consistently reward and evaluate, it is essential to make them the ones we prize most highly." The key phrase in this statement is "consistently reward and evaluate." The chances of being consistent in rewarding behavior diminish as one becomes less sure of goals. Unless we have given considerable thought to what behavior constitutes evidence of implicit change, we cannot claim to assess progress. Therefore, clarity in goal definition is critical.

We have frequently said that teaching is too vague and general and that a more systematic approach is needed. A system, in its broadest sense, can be thought of as the degree of order in one's approach to a task or problem. We might set up a continuum with random activity on one end and completely elaborated systems

at the other. Few educators would accept the notion that random activity was appropriate in their classrooms. Most would demand some degree of systematic planning. A problem may be simple or complex. The organization used to solve a problem may be ineffective (near the random end of our continuum) or effective (near the other end of our continuum). A system is an ordering of procedures needed to solve a task or a number of interrelated tasks. The degree of organization required increases as the number of tasks involved increases.

Ralph Tyler (1950) suggests four major components of a system: statement of objectives, criterion we are willing to accept as evidence of achievement of objectives, learning experiences selected to meet objectives, and final evaluation and revision procedures. These four are the necessary components of our completely elaborated system.

A. Cohen (1969) defines an objective as "a concrete criterion of achievement, measurable in terms of overt behavior." Mager (1962, p. 31) amplifies this definition: "An objective is an intent communicated by a statement describing a proposed change in a learner—a statement of what the learner is to be like when he has successfully completed a learning experience. It is a description of a pattern of behavior (performance) we want the learner to be able to demonstrate." Both Cohen (1969, p. 169) and Mager (1962, p. 12) see an objective as having three major sections: (1) task—what is one to *do?* (2) conditions—how broad or how specific must behavior or actions be in order to achieve the objective? (3) criteria —against what standards will behavior be evaluated to determine success in attaining the objective? Esbensen (1967) suggests that instructional objectives not be limited to specific teaching procedures. He argues that objectives should be stated in terms that permit the use of various teaching procedures.

Teaching can be considered the process of taking a learner through a series of carefully arranged sequences, each more sophisticated than the last, until the student has learned. Each step expands the learner's ability to integrate new perceptions into previous perceptions, apply his learnings, and use them to produce viable

47

and general solutions. The end of learning for the individual is increased independence from his environment. Specific behavioral objectives at each stage with constant, built-in evaluation enable both learner and teacher to monitor progress. Success provides incentive. The entire system then is cyclical and is unified about a single goal which is in turn divided into several objectives. The learner always knows where he is going and how far he has come. Objectives are organized according to various levels of intellectual difficulty and affective commitment (degree to which a student wants to do a task). The two dimensions (cognitive and affective) are hierarchically organized. These dimensions are interactive throughout the process. Higher degrees of commitment are expected as high-level cognitive skills are developed.

Individuals vary in their needs for information stores. Education should concentrate on maximizing the generative ability of each individual's store of learning plans. Systematic organization and clarity are essential, requiring specific behavioral objectives of varying levels of cognitive and affective difficulty. These levels represent different categories of cognitive ability and emotional sets. Behavioral objectives are the key to the entire learning process. The systems approach in implementing these objectives is the lock which the key opens.

The systems approach to planning is not new. All the components have been used by teachers and administrators for years. The new thing is the process—the way the four component parts are put together. Few teachers or administrators try to operate without systematic procedures. Yet, not many take the time to eliminate from their own behavior irrational (subjective) assumptions which affect the directions they select, the purposes they follow, the procedures they use, and the evaluations they make. The following is an example of a partially elaborated teaching system based on false assumptions. An instructor plans a course called Russian history. He establishes general objectives against which he can judge the intelligence of his group after they have completed the course. These objectives, which may or may not be known to the students, are helpful in justifying his efforts. He makes up a general-content out-

line which covers 1400 A.D. to the present. He selects a "good" text, one which will cause grades to be distributed in a normal bell-shaped curve. Enrollment and budget limitations may influence his decision. He divides the course into blocks so that the desired amount of material is covered in the fixed time available. The order of blocks probably follows the text. Lesson and unit plans are made out for class lectures. These plans may cover a whole semester or the instructor may keep a few chapters ahead of his students. If the course has been given before, the instructor may either modify previously used notes or simply leave them as they are and expect the students to know both text and notes. Tests are given at the end of each unit to see whether the students have mastered the material in the book and in the lectures. The test is graded on a normal curve. Special reviews and second chance tests are given to slow students.

The above example is based on widely accepted notions about the teaching-learning process. These notions hold that students must be taught a given volume of content. They also hold that instruction should be based on the average student and that testing is a sorting process. Our second example depicts a plan which might at best be termed irrational. The instructor does not outline his instruction plan more than a week or two ahead, if that. He jots down brief topics to be discussed. He believes this approach gives him flexibility in reacting to his students. He may also feel that extensive planning is a waste of his valuable time, which he can better use with his students. He gives the students a variety of different activities to keep them busy. Popham (1965, p. 8) notes of beginning teachers that their "decisions will often be based upon a rather simple motive—to fill the class hours with activities which *appear* (emphasis supplied) to be instructional." The instructor may be democratic in letting the students discuss what they want without regard for the topic of the lesson. He bases his tests on review questions and his own memory of topics covered in class. He cannot understand why his students do so poorly. The instructor likes certain students and not others and acts accordingly, but believes he is fair to all. At the end of the year, the instructor makes up a final exam based on what he thinks was covered in class. Often he has to "scale" the results to pass a reasonable number of students. If asked to give a careful review of his activities and objectives, he is in trouble and probably comes up with a fictitious summary. This second example pictures a teacher with vaguely defined concepts. Such a teacher is likely to view teaching as keeping students busy and showing that he cares (is a "regular guy" and "not too hard").

Definition and Application

Webster (1969, p. 895) defines system as "a regularly interacting or interdependent group of items forming a unified whole." The key words in this definition are "interacting group" and "unified whole." The loosely defined systems described above are not true systems because they are not integrated and unified. The first example was more-or-less integrated—lessons were planned in advance and connected—but since the purposes were not generally known to all participants, no unity existed. Stated purposes are essential to the systems approach. The evaluation based on them is equally important. Purposes—in terms of clearly-stated, behavioral change in learners—were added *after* the content outline had been established. Evaluation was a means of establishing a student's relative position (grade) rather than a means of checking fulfillment of objectives or the need to modify the learning process or the objectives.

In a systems approach, the purpose and all specific objectives must be known at the start, so that subsequent selection of processes and content or materials can be done with these purposes in mind. Final evaluation criteria are established at the same time the purposes and subpurposes are stated. No part of the system remains unless that part is effectively contributing to the achievement of the predetermined purposes. Evaluation is as much a process of system modification as it is a means of assessing final outcomes. A precise definition is given by Banathy (1968, p. 12):

> Systems are assemblages of parts that are designed and built by man into organized wholes for the attainment of specific purposes.

50

The purpose of a system is realized through processes in which interacting components of the system engage in order to produce a predetermined output. Purpose determines the process required, and the process will imply the kinds of components that will make up the system. A system receives its purpose, its input, its resources, and its constraints from its suprasystem. In order to maintain itself, a system has to produce an output which satisfies the suprasystem.

Banathy's definition introduces another element which must be considered in a general discussion of the systems approach applied to planning for total institutional change. This element is the suprasystem from which a system draws its nourishment and to which it must be responsive. The environment may be thought of as the ultimate suprasystem. Various subsystems, for instance education, make up the environment. Education may be divided into institutions of various types—four-year colleges, two-year colleges, secondary schools, and so forth. Two-year colleges can in turn be further subdivided into types, such as public and private, rural and urban, community colleges and technical institutes. Each institution can again be divided into departments and courses.

Each institution receives its input (students, goals, financial support, and so forth) from its immediate environment. It also sends students (output) into the environment and evaluates their success in terms of their ability to cope with it. If they are unsuccessful or only partly successful, adjustments in the program are necessary. The system can be thought of as a closed loop which is constantly self-adjusting. Presently, this somewhat ideal system has not been realized.

Earlier we mentioned the problem of social lag. Mort and Cornell (1941) found that approximately fifty years typically elapse between the identification of an educational need and the development and adoption of a solution. In 1964, Mort again found that "an extravagantly long time elapses before an insight into a need (or a discovery that practice is indefensible) is responded to by innovations destined for general acceptance." Miles (1964) suggested that incongruence between an innovation and a system at-

51

tempting the innovation may account, in part, for many innovative failures.

Much educational lag may be due to the failure of key institutional personnel to identify promising ideas and modify them to fit their particular institution. Typically they take the easy route—adopting a whole innovative system which is supported and endorsed by acknowledged experts. If the innovation fails, they blame the idea or the experts. It requires more effort to accept the essential ideas and then modify them to fit the particular situation. Ideas are evaluated (or at least should be) by college personnel in terms of their essential impact for improving individual student learning. Once an idea is considered promising, it must be systematically examined for relevance, implication, and projected effect. In this regard, community-college research efforts ought to be regarded as developmental. Although such an approach is a radical departure from present practice, the fundamental purpose of research efforts should be to enable college personnel to improve instructional effectiveness. Since no two communtiy colleges are identical, research efforts might be considered field-development research. This notion is essentially equivalent to the closed-loop feedback-evaluation system discussed earlier. The following eight steps are useful in implementing a systems approach for institutional change: identification of concerns, establishment of priorities, statement of the problem and objectives, identification of resources, environmental assessment, program design, program implementation, evaluation and revision.

Before briefly considering each of these steps, we must be sure that any change strategy is flexible enough to be valid for a wide range of educational problems, capable of constant on-site development, simple enough so that college personnel understand the process and can participate effectively in it, and sensitive to the interactive effects of any final decision.

This last point is particularly important. Every change has side effects. Persons using a systems approach must be careful to check these side effects to ensure that they are justified by the potential gain. As with a large beach ball which is less than fully inflated, a push on any part has an effect somewhere.

New Instructional Principles

In planning for educational change, the college must first determine the concerns of the societal groups it serves. For example, if the institution is in an upper-middle–class suburban location, a greater concern for college-level programs might be expected than in a college located in a major factory or heavy-manufacturing area. Once social needs are determined, institutional priorities can be established. The priorities ought to be based on consensus decisions of the contributing groups, and the goals of the institution should be realistic in terms of its resources. In simple terms, no one institution can do all things well. We agree with John Gardner's theme (1960) that a few things well done are preferable to many things done in a mediocre manner. Gardner's thesis may appear to contradict our earlier contention that two-year colleges should offer a variety of programs to meet the needs of their areas. A college may need to concentrate initially on major needs and incorporate low-priority needs later as institutional resources increase. A systematic survey of needs is the best guarantee of increasing effectiveness and community support.

Romine (1969, p. 5) argues that in defining institutional problems it is most important to "establish the contours and dimensions of the problem-producing situation and the tentative desired outcomes before solutions are attempted." If desired outcomes are not clearly stated in measurable terms at the beginning of the efforts, the program will lack an honest basis for ongoing evaluation. Often, outcomes (especially affective outcomes) are not initially stated in measurable terms. Consequently, the reports usually say something like the following: "There is no significant difference between team teaching and our present method of teaching, but we believe [guess!] that favorable attitudes toward school are being developed by team teaching." A plan for measuring such "attitudes" in advance eliminates such vague conclusions. The report might also show that the innovation had less impact than first press releases indicated.

Once the goal or problem has been specifically stated in measurable terms, information must be gathered. At this point, many institutions short-circuit their change strategies. The institution must fully investigate published data on the proposed change,

53

both in terms of its theoretical basis and practical applications. It must also assess the specific institutional environment. In what ways does the environment suggest modifications or limitations of other programs? Too often, omission of self-analysis results in mistakes which develop only after much time and money have been expended. Later changes are then likely to be resisted since participants may feel they are wasting their time again. Designing a program requires making a decision which is "at once a conclusion and a hypothesis" (Romine, 1969, p. 6). The decision is a conclusion in the sense that it is based on information gathered in earlier phases. It is also a hypothesis in the sense that modifications have been made and behavioral outcomes have been predicted. The program, once set, must be constantly evaluated against predetermined criteria to ensure that it is moving toward the desired outcomes. Such comprehensive evaluation quickly identifies weaknesses before they become major problems. It also provides evidence of positive environmental elements which may be used as bases for later changes, and it involves a wide range of personnel. Hopefully the personnel will develop an awareness of the process of systematic change and a commitment to it. Once a particular program has been formulated, participants must know what they are to do, know to whom they are responsible and the task deadlines to be met, and know what the limits of their authority are. Often, a solid program is confounded by lack of attention to these details.

Although evaluation and revision are the final steps in the process, they have been going on all along. Final program evaluation requires data from earlier evaluations. The purpose is to compare actual program outcomes with expected program outcomes. Such an assessment should include affective as well as cognitive or material outcomes. After the final evaluations are completed, revisions in the program should be made. Changes may have an effect on the needs and priorities of the institution, thus generating a new change cycle.

The foregoing discussion illustrates one way to implement a systems approach at the institutional level. The remainder of this chapter presents models of systems approach at the classroom level.

The process at this level is compatible with the administrative process described above. Such compatibility is essential to the maintenance of unity between the suprasystem (the institution) and its sub-system (individual classrooms). Compatibility does not mean, however, that change in the classroom cannot be made without general institutional change. But such efforts are difficult without institutional support.

In considering the systems approach at the classroom or instructional level, we find the same basic elements noted in our discussion of the systems approach applied to institutional change. Table 2 presents an abbreviated comparison of the traditional and nontraditional approaches. The basic elements are objectives, criterion levels of learner performance, learning activities, and evaluation and revision procedures. These basic components can be ordered in many ways. Let us look at a few of the current systems. All begin with a statement of purpose. All require a set of criteria against which progress can be measured. All are sensitive to the content and processes used in instructional sequences. All evaluate progress in terms of specific behaviorally stated objectives. Evaluation is usually seen as final and as procedural (used to determine the initial position of learners and to modify the entire system). The hallmark of any system is its proven capability for producing measurable learning achievement.

Models

Banathy regards the instructional system as a closed loop. Feedback evaluation reenters the system at all phases. Objectives are the starting point in Banathy's structure (see Figure 1), and the criterion or evaluation test is based on them. Learning tasks are analyzed to determine which will achieve a given objective. After the analysis, the initial competence or entering abilities of the learner are assessed. Then the particular learning tasks are formulated. In the next step, the content and the processes which will best enable the learner to accomplish the specific learning tasks are analyzed. Finally, the system is tested on learners and the initial objectives are evaluated. The system may then be modified at any stage. This

Table 2. INSTRUCTIONAL SYSTEMS

Teaching-Oriented System (Traditional)	*Learning-Oriented System (Nontraditional)*
PROCESSES	
A. Instruction is unsystematized.	A. Instructional technology undergirds entire system.
B. Groups are instructed under controlled conditions.	B. Instruction is individualized.
C. Teacher presentation is equated with learning. Whatever has been covered in class is considered learned by student.	C. Teaching has not occurred unless student has learned.
D. Objectives are vague and general.	D. Objectives are specific and measurable.
E. Audio-visuals are used as aids to teaching.	E. Media are used not as a supplement but as a component of teaching, selected on basis of potential to cause student learning.
F. Only "essential" knowledge is dealt with.	F. Content is chosen on basis of its relevance.
G. Testing is used to categorize students.	G. Testing is used to assess teaching.
H. Teacher is the actor; students the audience. Teacher controls selection of objectives, content, and learning experiences; student simply reacts.	H. Student is the actor; teacher the manager. Students participate in selection of objectives, content, and learning experiences.
ENVIRONMENT	
Uniform and regulated; thirty students per teacher; fifty-minute class periods; eighteen-week semesters or eleven-week quarters	Freedom prevails; flexible student-teacher ratio, flexible period length and scheduling, flexible semester

Source: Roueche and Herrscher (1970).

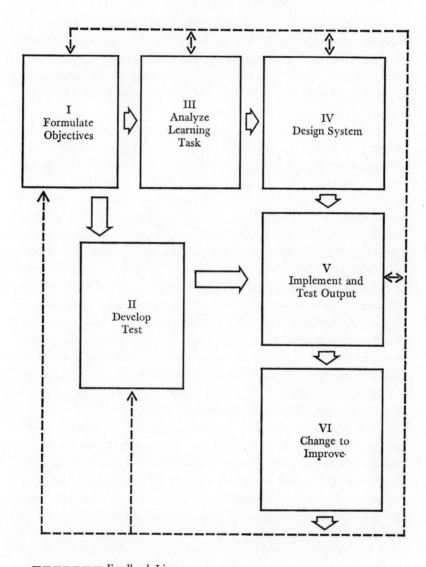

------- Feedback Line

FIGURE 1.   Banathy's Model. Source: Banathy, 1968.

model separates the analysis of learning tasks from the analysis of content and processes. It also includes a preassessment of student abilities. One of the strengths of the Banathy's model is that it systematically considers each objective in terms of sublearnings or skills. When used along with a pretest, this procedure should prevent gaps in the sequence of instruction.

Kemp has also designed an instructional systems model (Figure 2) with a similar ordering of elements. This model makes separate elements of some of Banathy's subcomponents. Kemp includes a general purpose distinct from behavioral objectives. The general purpose is stated first. The specific behavioral objectives follow later. In this approach, content is separated from process. Preassessment of student abilities occurs between the selection of content and the process of instruction. In our opinion, this system may endanger integration of content and process. In selecting content, the teacher might unwittingly limit instructional methods. By considering content and processes together he can reduce this danger. Kemp, like Banathy, views evaluation as part of a closed loop. Unlike Banathy's model, however, Kemp's model separates the pretest from the objectives. Kemp also introduces a new aspect omitted by Banathy, namely business matters such as budget and personnel. In our opinion business matters are an important consideration, particularly in planning for a large group of students.

Popham (Figure 3) combines many of the elements in the two preceding models and shows that the teacher draws his objectives from many sources. Popham's model also suggests that information is screened by the teacher in terms of his knowledge of learning psychology and his philosophy of education. In this respect, Popham's model ties in closely with our emphasis on the importance of a set philosophy and learning principles. A strong subjective element exists in any instructional system no matter how objective the model may appear. Popham's model calls attention to the sources of objectives at the outset. The remaining phases of the model are similar to those in the Banathy model. A final criterion test is implied under Point 2 of "objectives." A preassessment is made. Learning activities again combine content with instructional processes.

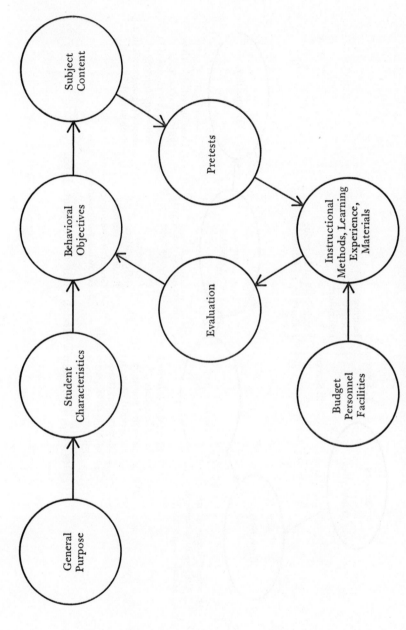

FIGURE 2. Kemp's Model. Source: Kemp, 1969.

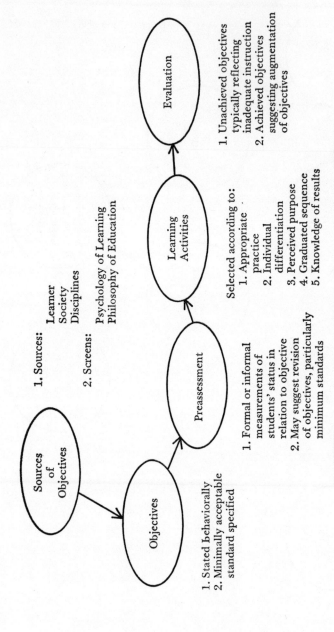

FIGURE 3. Popham's Model. Source: Popham, 1965.

Evaluation in Popham's model is seen as final. We feel that this finality is a limitation. We suggest a closed loop with an arrow from evaluation to objectives.

The final model we discuss was proposed by Herrscher (1970). Figure 4 presents this instructional system, which we feel is most appropriate for community-college instruction. It embodies

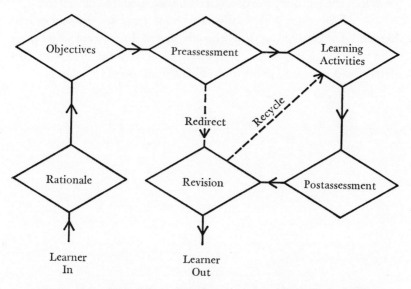

FIGURE 4. Herrscher's Model. Source: Herrscher, 1970.

the best features of the preceding models. In this model, "rationale" is synonymous with Popham's "source of objectives." "Learning activities" integrates content and processes. Postassessment is seen as summative and as a means for revision. In addition, the model shows a two-way movement at the revision stage. If the learner is successful, he moves out of the loop after providing information which may assist revision. If he is unsuccessful, he is recycled for additional learning activities. Both positive and negative feedback are obtained, and revision becomes a process of correcting weaknesses and expanding strengths.

Two additions might be made to this model. First, business

considerations (budget, personnel, and so on) could be added at the learning-activities point. More important, we feel a need for revision or introduction of objectives (to be indicated by another dotted line going from the revision stage to the objectives stage). This process would make allowance for a situation in which few students, if any, met a given objective. In that situation, rather than recycling the learners, the objective may be modified or deleted.

All the models show a systematic attempt to structure teaching and learning around specifically stated behavioral objectives. The model is effective only if it produces behavioral change in predetermined ways and provides feedback at all points.

5

Motivating Students

The two-year community college is a unique institution designed for a special purpose—catering to a nontraditional student body. It is committed to the highest caliber of instruction and is expected to *teach*. However, these noble aims are far from being realized, and a great deal of traditional thinking prevails in most community colleges.

We have suggested that the present philosophical base is restricted. We constructed our own philosophical base to encompass the aims of all students. Attention was focused on the individual learner, not the group. The increased ability of each individual to operate in and on his environment was our goal for all students. We also suggested that current operational procedures are too vague. They must be clearly stated and systematically implemented at all levels of the institution's operation. We argued that systematic instruction can fill this need.

We defined learning as a change in behavior. Instruction, then, is the deliberate attempt to cause change in learners by means of predetermined behavioral objectives. These concepts have value

63

in community colleges if it can be shown that all (or nearly all) students can learn. This chapter presents Bloom's concept of mastery learning and its implications for community-college organization.

Basic Assumptions

Bloom (1968) says: "Most students (perhaps over 90 per cent) can master what we have to teach them. . . . As we study aptitude distributions in relation to student performance, we have become convinced that there are differences between the extreme students and the remainder of the population." He concludes that some students in the top 1 to 5 per cent of the aptitude range have special talent in a given subject. Whether this talent is the result of previous training or of native endowment is unclear. At the other end of the aptitude distribution "there are individuals with special disabilities for particular learning." Bloom maintains that this group "may constitute less than 5 per cent of the distribution, but this will vary with the subject and the aptitudes." The disabilities Bloom refers to are fixed—either mental or physical.

Bloom contends that the normal grading curve is nonvalid. Standardized tests built on national norms are designed to produce a normal distribution of scores. Such distribution is based on large numbers and random distribution. The purpose of a systems approach is to reduce chance effects. Therefore, we would expect the distribution in the systems approach to be fixed. Bloom says, "We may even insist that our educational efforts have been unsuccessful to the extent to which our distribution of achievement approximates the normal distribution." The tradition of grading on a normal curve is the major weakness of many present attempts to recognize individual differences. A teacher may tailor his efforts to fit individual needs and even give special activities to students. However, if the grade given at the end of a course is based on a normal curve distribution, individual differences have not truly been recognized.

Variables

Bloom defines five major variables in learning: aptitude for particular kinds of learning, quality of instruction, ability to understand instruction, perseverance, and time allowed for learning. Let us first consider aptitude for learning. Because the aptitude tests given at the beginning of a course generally correlate as high as +.70 with achievement measures at the end of a course, high levels of achievement are possible only for the most able students. Carroll (1963) presents a different concept. He says that "aptitude is the amount of time required by the learner to attain mastery of a learning task." Bloom extends the implicit assumption in the above idea and says: "Given enough time, all students can conceivably attain mastery of a learning task." The key problem is "enough time." When does the teacher reach the point of diminishing returns? Is time the only determinant? Other factors such as motivation and native endowments surely enter in. A. Cohen (1969, p. 47) discusses this problem and concludes "that the problem may be merely semantical and require the concession that other variables do affect learning mastery for students. But the point is that this particular definition of aptitude is not necessary to Bloom's thesis on learning mastery strategies and its redefinition need not negate his consequent assumption that given sufficient time all students may be able to achieve mastery." The problem is greatly simplified if the lowest 5 per cent are excluded from consideration.

The notion of quality of instruction is based upon the assumption that there is a standard classroom situation for all students. This assumption has greatly influenced education. Such an assumption is the antithesis of our teaching-learning rationale and implies that the evaluative standard for all educational endeavor is the group; effective teaching is based on group standards. Constant attempts are made to find the best program, curriculum, teaching technique, and so on for a given group. One wonders why the investigators conducting these consistently unsuccessful attempts have not abandoned their premise. How can group-referenced research flourish at the same time educators demand attention to individual differences?

Carroll (1963) suggests a new premise based on the individual learner. He defines instruction "in terms of the degree to which the presentation, explanation, and ordering of elements of the task to be learned approach the optimum for a given learner." But what is optimum for various learners? There can be no best group answer. Bloom tells us that "the quality of instruction is to be considered in terms of its effects on individual learners rather than on random groups of learners." Bloom concludes that because high-quality tutors for each student are economically impossible, alternative schemes are needed. We feel that the systems approach has the potential to be a satisfactory alternative.

Each student must have "the ability . . . to understand the nature of the task he is to learn and the procedures he is to follow in the learning of the task" (Bloom, 1968). In the traditional class-room, the student encounters a single teacher using a single set of instructional materials. These materials are adequate if the learner understands the teacher and the materials. However, the student is in serious trouble if he does not. A variety of instructional methods must be used to accommodate various learning styles and interests. Our review of learning principles illustrated the need for developing various systems of thought: imagerial, action, and symbolic.

Bloom suggests that group study, tutoring, textbooks, work-books and programed-instruction units, audio-visual methods, and academic games all should be considered because no one of these is ideal for all learners. The aim is to find the technique in which "the student's abilities interact with the instructional material and the instructor's abilities in teaching" (Bloom, 1968).

We have repeatedly mentioned that nontraditional practices are needed to fit the needs of nontraditional students. Too fre-quently, instruction stresses symbolic systems and almost guaranties failure for low verbal-ability students—a sizable portion of the com-munity college population. "For the student in our highly verbal schools it is likely that this ability to understand instruction is primarily determined by verbal ability and reading comprehension" (Bloom, 1968). He further notes that "while it is possible to alter an individual's verbal ability by appropriate training (vocabulary and reading ability) there are limits to the amount of change that can be produced." Too often designers of innovative materials fail to consider that the underlying difficulty is a deficiency in verbal skills. How often have you gone to an instructor to ask for clarification of an idea and been given additional reading which only confused you further? Clearly, instructors must offer alternative styles of materials, not just alternative content.

Carroll (1963) defines perseverance as "the time the learner is willing to spend in learning." Students vary in the amount of perseverance they bring to a specific learning task. If the task is enjoyable, the student may have considerable perseverance (a boy working on his car). If it is unpleasant, he may quickly leave the task (the same boy studying English grammar). More formally, Bloom states: "As a student finds the effort rewarding, he is likely to spend more time on a particular learning task." Bloom also notes that one can try to "increase the amount of perseverance in students, [but] it is likely that manipulation of the instruction and learning materials may be more effective in helping students master a learning task, in spite of their present level of perseverance. . . . As students attain mastery of a given task, they are likely to increase their perseverance for a related learning task."

Why should learning be made so difficult that only a small portion of the students can persevere to mastery? Parkinson's Law apparently applies to many educational situations. Parkinson's Law states that the amount of time available for a given task is directly proportional to the amount of time believed necessary for the task. Think of the times you had a term paper to do. Think of the actual time you spent on it after putting it off until the last week. Probably you accomplished your task. Perhaps you even got a high grade. The time required to do most tasks can be drastically reduced by careful planning and systematic arrangement of materials. Careful planning and manipulation of procedures can give teachers additional time for slow learners, can accelerate fast learners, and can reduce the degree of perseverance demanded by difficult or confusing material.

The time needed by various students to complete a task differs. Therefore, "the student must not only devote the amount of time he needs to the learning task but also be allowed enough time for learning" (Bloom, 1968). Bloom also suggests that we presently

67

waste too much time. "If instruction and student use of time become more effective . . . most students will need less time to learn the subject to mastery and . . . the ratio of time required for the slower and the faster learners may be reduced from about 6 to 1 to perhaps 3 to 1. Bloom also observes "a zero or a slightly negative relationship between final grades and the amount of time spent on homework." One possible explanation for such findings is that, if assigned materials are inappropriate or confusing, the student gains nothing from them except possibly a store of memorized items. Bloom (1968) summarizes his strategy as follows:

> We are convinced that it is not the sheer amount of time spent in learning (either in school or out of school) that accounts for the level of learning. We believe that each student should be allowed the time he needs to learn a subject. And, the time he needs to learn the subject is likely to be affected by the student's aptitudes, his verbal ability, the quality of instruction he receives in class, and the quality of the help he receives outside of class. The task of a strategy for mastery learning is to find ways of altering the time individual students need for learning as well as to find ways of providing whatever is needed by each student. Thus, a strategy for mastery learning must find some way of solving the instructional problems as well as the school organizational (including time) problems.

Organizational Problems

The reader may wonder why mastery learning applied through the systems approach has not been widely accepted and implemented. Such a program is revolutionary and challenges most traditional concepts of higher education. Change comes about slowly, and overcoming educational inertia is no easy matter. Mastery learning through a systems approach calls for a high degree of commitment, expertise, and cooperation. Educational personnel must become accountable for student learning. Educators have been slow in accepting the notion of accountability. Accountability is seldom part of teacher promotion and tenure practices.

Carlson (1965, p. 4) points out that "part of the explanation of the slow rate of change in public schools . . . lies with the absence of an institutionalized change agent . . . in public education. A *change agent* . . . can be defined as a person who attempts to influence the adoption of decisions in a direction he feels is desirable. He is a professional who has as his major function the advocacy and introduction of innovations into practices." The two key words are *decisions* and *innovations*. The first implies positive leadership toward (and responsibility for) causing learning. The second should be understood as innovations consistent with the overall change strategy of the institution.

The Committee for Economic Development (1968, pp. 29–30) notes that research is too seldom used. It suggests that the reason is that "within the schools themselves there are few people who are qualified to analyze research findings even if these were made readily available. Nor are there any people in the school system capable of aiding teachers and administrators in converting these findings into practical use." Research-and-development specialists are needed to implement change strategies. Considerable research information on the process and necessary conditions for learning is available. Our own teaching-learning rationale has been developed from what we feel is the most promising of such research. Much is known about the development of instructional objectives, strategies, and materials. However, the trained personnel who must implement the new strategies are missing. Miles (1964) comments: "Almost all available funds, energy and time [have] gone into the development of innovations as such. The fraction available for examination of, planning for, and sophisticated execution of change processes seems to be minor." A change strategy and an innovation are not synonymous. An innovation is an isolated idea which may or may not be useful to a given institution. Before it can be incorporated into a change strategy, it must be examined for relevance, become integrated into the overall planning process of an individual institution, and be clearly and effectively executed. Implementing change strategies—a set of innovations—is a major problem. We are suggesting the reorganization of the entire educational process, beginning with its underlying philosophy and building on learning principles which are not widely implemented. Bloom's mastery learning program is still threatening to many educators. The program is predicated upon systematic organizational support, which is vaguely understood by most community-college administrators and trustees. Change strategies and the key people needed to implement them will become available as educational laboratories develop programs and train specialists and classroom teachers in the systems approach and Bloom's mastery learning. Several major universities are now training such personnel.

Accountability

Accountability is the single most important concept in implementing the educational changes proposed in preceding chapters. This concept affects the entire organization and all of the personnel of an educational institution. Accountability is a corollary to learning for mastery. This relationship must hold since, if 95 per cent of our students can learn, teachers must accept the responsibility for such learning. Accountability is more than a glib term which elicits strong feelings from teachers. The concept is grounded in the belief that public educational institutions exist to serve the communities that support them and must therefore shoulder the responsibility for their students. Public disenchantment with the poor job that education has been doing has enhanced the need for such responsibility. Former Commissioner of Education James Allen (1970) observes: "The people have a right to be assured that the increasingly large investments in education that will be called for will produce results. They can no longer be expected to be satisfied with definitions of school quality that focus primarily on such factors as per-pupil expenditures, teacher-pupil ratios, and teacher salary levels." Accountability is a practical method for confronting some of our most critical educational dilemmas, including the reestablishment of public confidence in education.

Community colleges are often referred to as "democracy's colleges"—the result of social demands for educational opportunity for all citizens. They are more closely identified with local social needs than are other institutions of higher education. However, the idea that an institution, even a community college, hold itself accountable for student learning is not widely accepted. Instead, that responsibility still weighs heavily on the student. Students have long been accountable for what they have or have not learned. The new approach turns the tables and makes the schools and teachers equally responsible for student performance.

We suggest that community-college administrators stop counting the number of volumes in the library or measuring the square footage per full-time student, and start examining how well students are being taught. Accountability has gained most attention through the "performance contracts." In this system a private company contracts with a school system to run a learning program. The company guaranties that the students will reach particular objectives within a specified time. The company is then paid according to how well the students are able to perform. If the students do not learn, the school board is not required to reimburse the contractor.

Soon after the Texarkana, Arkansas, school system awarded a dropout-prevention performance contract to Dorsett Educational Systems—a private, profit-making firm—school boards in Texas, Michigan, California, and Oregon quickly followed suit (*Education Turnkey News*). Today, scores of private companies are ready to take on such contracts. The easy optimism of these companies contrasts sharply with the complaint of professional educators that better programs require more money. The companies say, "We can teach them." Teachers say, "We can't; they are poorly motivated, have poor attitudes, and we need more money in order to deal with them." Are more money (or better students) fundamental solutions to effectiveness?

Fortunately educators have begun to question long-accepted instructional and administrative modes of procedure (for example, the lecture method; the predetermined amount of material to be covered in a given period of time; the excessive reliance upon books as a learning resource, and the organization of learning activities into academic years, semesters, hours, credits, and grade-point averages. All these procedures constitute restrictions on the learning process. We contend that accountability for student learning is necessary and

71

that the means are now available to train teachers and administrators to implement it.

Since 1967 the National Laboratory for Higher Education (NLHE)—formerly Regional Education Laboratory for the Carolinas and Virginia (RELCV)—has developed training programs designed to implement educational change. The NLHE junior- and community-college program specifies that:

(1) Institutionwide policy shall be adopted which states that faculty and administrators shall be accountable for student learning. (2) Nonpunitive grading procedures shall be adopted (e.g., incompletes do not convert to F's, credit-noncredit system used, etc.). (3) Registration and enrollment procedures shall be modified to accommodate for varying rates of completion of the instructional program. (4) Instructor evaluation shall be made on the basis of student achievement.

This program also calls for an instructional climate where it is safe to try new things, communication is open, all members participate in decision-making, formal leaders are supportive of instruction, all are dedicated to the basic job of student learning and public accountability, and people cooperate to get the job done.

Community-college personnel must accept causing learning as their primary aim. All activities must be evaluated against this goal. Activities which cannot be clearly related to improving student learning must be reconsidered and possibly phased out. The most obvious example of the way this goal affects institutional procedures is in policy statements. Rules abound in most educational institutions. Colleges have set up student regulations, teacher regulations, administrative policies, board policies, and so on. Often, many so-called policies are unwritten or are hopelessly out of date. Aside from providing work for policy formulators (administrative assistants, deans of students, and so on) and providing printing contracts, such policies usually collect dust on shelves. Reevaluation of policies would produce at least two results: improved communications and reduced confusion and improved student morale. Student grievances (potential sources of student activism) are reduced and become difficult to sustain if the administration can honestly show that

72

policies and rules are designed to assist learning rather than to constrict freedom of choices and actions.

A unified purpose also assists personnel to clarify their functions and reestablish priorities among themselves and to the public. The public is being asked to support education with hard cash and is often refusing. We cannot ignore public relations. Colleges which have unclear goals and priorities typically reflect this confusion to the public.

Grading

Noncompetitive grading is essential in our approach. Students entering community colleges typically come from institutions with traditional grading systems. Two-year students going on to four-year institutions will generally reenter institutions using these systems. A revision of the community-college grading system therefore presents a two-fold problem. The first problem is evaluating the incoming student's previous education. Currently, a guidance counselor administers several tests, checks past records, and directs the student to the program he feels the student can handle. Sometimes, the guidance office places him in the program of his choice, whether appropriate or not, on the assumption that everyone has the right to fail. Frequently, they direct him to a remedial program which, if successfully completed, will eventually allow him to enroll in the program he desires. Past grades must not be considered absolute predictors of success or failure under a noncompetitive mastery system. We are not suggesting that previous grades give the school no usable information. Past grades may indicate which students are verbal and are independent learners. However, placement or admission to programs based on these grades alone is not valid under a mastery system.

The ideal curriculum, according to the mastery concept, offers a variety of programs divided into units with set objectives. Each unit begins at the elementary level and increases in difficulty. The student elects the courses he desires, takes pretests, and is placed at whatever level he can handle. Remediation is not seen as a separate program below college level but is integrated into the programs. The student should be told what his chances are in any program. Colleges can develop their own norms and tests to measure the abilities required for success in their programs rather than using national norms to assess student potential. Instructors should be assisted to develop units of instruction which accommodate learning weakness.

Once a student is admitted to a given program, he should be graded according to his ability. Each course must have stated behavioral objectives against which each individual's progress can be measured. The time allowed to accomplish any set of objectives must be left open to allow for individual learning rates. The instructor may use a credit/no credit grading system or an A, B, C letter-grade system. In the first system, the learner either passes the final examination and receives credit for the course, or he receives nothing. If he does not pass the final examination, he continues working until he achieves the required course objectives. In the A, B, C system, three performance levels are established. The student can work for any grade. If he tries for an A and fails, he can try again or accept a lower grade. If he fails to perform at the C level, he receives no credit. Although this concept of grades is difficult for faculty to accept initially, many community colleges have abolished all punitive grades—D's and F's.

If grading practices are untraditional, will students have difficulty in transferring to institutions with traditional systems? Our first-hand inquiries have revealed that institutions willing to explain their programs, provide evidence of student achievement, and discuss their programs with four-year personnel encounter no difficulties in transferring their students. The total testing function is seen, therefore, as primarily diagnostic and supportive, not as a procedure for student classification.

Course Patterns

Community colleges encounter difficulty when considering ways to accommodate varying rates of learning. If aptitude is a function of time, and individual learning rates vary, the college must make an effort to allow for everyone to learn at his own rate. The quick student should not be held back or given busy work. The slow student must be given more time rather than watered-down learning sequences or failing grades. Administrators must provide flexible scheduling for course length and class hours. Secondary and elementary schools are recognizing this fact. Varying group size (from individual study to large-group instruction), nongraded schools, flexible credit requirements, and modular scheduling of class periods have all been tried. (Modular scheduling is based on concepts common to several courses as opposed to strict scheduling on X days per week at Y o'clock without reference to subject organization.) Participating students demonstrated improved retention and increased their achievement level. Traditional time periods or class patterns are not sacred.

The systems approach is ideally suited to the need for flexibility. Once behavioral objectives are established and individual learning units are developed, students are free to work on these units individually or in small groups. Feedback from systems evaluation should help reduce wasted instruction time. The time saved through effective and efficient instruction provides flexibility in scheduling and program content without adding personnel and increasing costs.

Learning styles and interests vary as well as learning rates. Bloom (1968) and Carroll (1963) focus particularly on the ability of the student to understand instruction. They advocate the use of a variety of instructional methods and argue that instructional sequences offering the learner alternative methods are desirable and probably essential. How far can a college follow this program? The size and resources of the institution and its resources, both personnel and equipment, are important factors. Cohen (1969) describes an ideal situation.

> The college offers six distinctly different types of instructional sections in each course [though not for each unit]. Each section has its own reason and style; each one is based on a specific instructional form—yet all sections lead to similar course goals. The six types of sections offered in each course are categorized by the different media employed. Those varied media are not simply different reading lists or types of lectures given by different

people; each one is a disinct design for instruction [we have called this instructional system] that is built on a distinct rationale. Most units in each course are offered in lecture, discussion, independent-study, tutorial, audio-tutorial, and computer-assisted sections. The sections run concurrently throughout the year in staggered time sequences.

Under this system, students can shift from one section into another with no loss of credit if one style proves inappropriate. Students may come and go as they wish. Credit is based upon the number of units passed. Record-keeping is simplified because the registrar enters only courses completed on the student's transcript. The registrar plays no role until the student receives course credit.

This system, which allows students to shift sections at will, is crucial. If the goal of instruction is mastery and if time limitations are dropped, then the program must include horizontal and vertical flexibility. (By horizontal mobility, we mean the freedom of the student to move about from program to program within the school. By vertical mobility we mean his freedom to move as fast as he wishes.) Traditional tracks are eliminated. We are not suggesting that each student be on his own with no direction or assistance. Guidance personnel are responsible for informing the students of college requirements. However, the student, once informed, is free to choose his program. This system places the burden of course and program articulation where it belongs—squarely on the shoulders of the administrative personnel.

In our system, an instructor's success is measured in terms of his student's success in achieving behavioral objectives. Merit pay is the subject of much debate in the literature. Many contend that such a system is impossible because no one agrees on what constitutes effective teaching or how it can best be measured. In discussing this problem, Cohen and Brawer (1969) conclude that the fault of present teacher evaluation systems lies in their narrow scope. They are based on teacher performance in the classroom only. They fail to define adequately what constitutes teaching. The raters' ideas of teaching are equated with personal goodness, which may or may not have anything to do with effectiveness. Cohen and Brawer suggest

76

that evaluation of teachers is only valid when it relates to institutional goals and reasonable criteria. Such criteria are the instructors' own behavioral objectives.

Several community colleges across the nation have developed faculty contracts and faculty-evaluation techniques that place proper focus on learning and student performance. The teacher is in a supporting role. A faculty employment contract (Appendix A) developed by Robert S. Zimmer, president of Passaic County Community College, Wayne, New Jersey, incorporates the ideas presented in this text. The contract is also consistent with the recommendations of Cohen and Brawer. The evaluation rationale is simple: Faculty promotions are based on the ability of the instructor to produce measurable learning in increasing numbers of students.

Personnel

We have discussed the need for a comprehensive change of educational strategy in order to implement mastery learning. The Passaic County Community College employment and promotion policy illustrates the scope of changes necessary. Such major changes will not be realized without dynamic leadership and the professional assistance of community-college leaders. Administrators cannot expect faculty to show the way. They must persuade the faculty and assist them to incorporate mastery learning into their procedures. Brown and Mayhew (1965, p. 56) emphasize the need for administrative action: "College faculty members are typically conservative with respect to the essential educational content and mission of their institutions. It is difficult to think of an important curricular innovation that was originated and put into effect by faculty members operating in their corporate capacities."

Where will the impetus for change originate? We see three sources: the college board of trustees, the president, and an agent called the educational development officer (EDO). Other key administrators such as deans, guidance personnel, vice-presidents, department heads, and so forth, can introduce innovation as well. However, the board, the president, and the educational development officer are in the best position.

A Modest Proposal: Students Can Learn

Historically, college trustees have deferred to administrators on most educational matters. Board members spend much time attending meetings (full board meetings, committee meetings, and special meetings of college groups), making speeches on behalf of the college, soliciting funds, recruiting students, and holding personal conferences with college personnel (Rauh, 1969, pp. 6–7).

Newburn (1964) refers to the relationship between trustees and administrators as the same as that between amateurs and "pros." The trustees are laymen. They assume that the educators whom they have selected (the "pros") know best how to organize, administer, and evaluate the college. Board members have seldom seen their role in terms of contributing to the development of learning and teaching—the essence of the community college.

Cohen and Roueche (1969) found that few community college presidents are assigned educational responsibilities by the boards of trustees. Even more disconcerting, they found that few presidents regularly report to the trustees on educational matters. The traditional, typical president, like the mechanic who keeps the educational machine running smoothly, is left with the task of campus planning, selection of staff, organizational development, community and public relations, fund-raising, and keeping his own position secure. Rarely does the president directly influence the development of an educational climate in an attempt to provide maximum learning benefits for students. Even more rarely does the president question the success of a program once it has been established. Presidents mostly defer to their deans on educational matters. The title *dean of instruction* seems to imply responsibility for the educational program and instruction. However, an examination of the activities and duties of the typical dean of instruction indicates that he spends most of his time filling out forms, writing the college catalog, developing a faculty handbook, scheduling classes, signing student excuses, and attending to faculty and student grievances. The instructional dean in most colleges is concerned with everything *except* instruction.

The board of trustees (who establish the goals of the college) must also be responsible for the achievements of the college. It is their job to find out what progress is being made toward those goals. Griffiths (1964) observes that the major impetus for change in organizations comes from the outside. The degree and duration of change are directly proportional to the amount of pressure applied. The governing board is the outside organization having the closest and most consistent interaction with the community college. Its expectations of the college in general and the president in particular are potential powerful elements of change. Expectations can be given substantive form in terms of policy statements and actions which ask the right questions of the president and require answers. Boards should create an environment in which presidents must become educational leaders to retain their positions. For example, boards should inquire regularly into the following educational matters: What percentage of the young people in the community attend the college? What percentage of the young people in the community attend no postsecondary-school educational institution? What percentage of those enrolled leave before completing one term? What percentage leave before completing the program for which they enrolled? Why do they leave? What measures are being taken to reduce the attrition rate? Where do students go when they leave school? What jobs do they take? Do they attend other educational institutions?

Other questions are perhaps even more crucial for making an institution accountable:

(1) What can we expect our students to be able to do after completing a course at the college? This question, as we have previously suggested, requires that college teachers develop specific, measurable objectives for the courses they teach. If we define teaching as causing learning, we are simply asking the teachers (the "pros," remember) to state in advance what their students will be able to do after successfully completing their courses.

(2) What programs are being developed to make instructors effective in causing students to learn? Teachers, for the most part, have not been prepared to teach. They are subject-matter experts with few ideas on how to cause student learning. Trustees must ensure that colleges develop effective in-service training activi-

ties in order for teachers to become skilled and proficient in producing learning. Proper allocation of budget resources is an important consideration.

(3) Have appropriate learning activities been provided for all students? Many of the students who enter community colleges are nearly illiterate (especially those in the adult basic-education programs) or desperately deficient in communications skills. Audiovisual materials can help students who are lost in a lecture or reading course. The conventional lecture is ill-suited to the majority of students who enter the community college.

Asking questions is not enough. Administrators must answer. Tendler and Wilson (1970, pp. 11–12) insist:

> Merely to ask the right questions is hardly enough. Board members should encourage periodic presentations by the students, faculty, and staff. Boards should keep continuing records of questions asked, answers provided, reports requested, and reports received. Only if board members are meticulous in their record-keeping can they measure the performance of the college. Each question must be satisfactorily answered, each report must be delivered where requested and contain the necessary information. If such a check is not maintained, the entire procedure is liable to be worthless. Under such circumstances a competent president will welcome the opportunity to keep his board informed for he is then assured, on a continuing basis, that they understand what the college program is all about and he need not consume his energies with "handling" the board on the basis of charm, personality, or subterfuge. An incompetent president will be pressured rather than assisted by his format.

Can boards operate in this suggested manner? Several community-college boards have adopted strong positions on institutional accountability. The trustees at John Tyler Community College (Chester, Virginia), for example, require the president to report periodically on the following: (1) the success of students in attaining course objectives (including attrition and failure rates); (2) the success of students in occupations assumed upon leaving the college (including the employer's evaluation of the college programs); (3) the success of students who transfer to other institutions; (4)

the success in attaining the stated aims of the college (John Tyler Community College, Local Board Resolution, 1969).

The John Tyler Community College Board formulated a resolution committing the institution to a policy of accountability and developed a set of guidelines for the selection of a president. They wished to be sure that the key leader, the president, was willing to go on record in support of such a policy. The policy is included in Appendix B in its entirety to show how one board has asked the right questions and assumed an active role in educational leadership.

The president must ultimately accept the responsibility for bringing about educational change in the community college. The setting is right for him to provide the impetus for change. Research has shown that change in organizations frequently comes from the top down (Griffiths, 1964, pp. 524–536). Jencks (1965, pp. 17–21) observes that most college administrators are extremely sympathetic to curricular innovation. However, innovation does not happen by itself. The president, like the board members, must inquire regularly into the educational programs of his institution. How he chooses to do so can vary from institution to institution. Whether he chooses to do so is another matter. In general, administrators have been rewarded for doing nothing; that is, they have maintained the status quo and caused no problems for the board. The community continues to support the institution, students continue to enroll, and the faculty remain complacent. From a business standpoint this policy is sound management. However, it has little in common with educational leadership.

No enterprise can succeed unless the president cooperates. He may choose not to lead; yet he retains the authority to keep others from leading. The community-college president can make a career of managing and never get around to leading. He may never realize that he is doing one and not the other. The president must be reoriented to initiate change himself and to support the legitimate efforts of others.

The president must know where his college is going and how it can realize its mission without getting detoured. He must set the climate—a climate dedicated to causing learning. The president must be proficient in mastery learning and the systems approach. He must know the difference between administratrivia and effective administrative practices. Finally, he must be open to his staff and demonstrate that democratic processes, cooperation, and the ideas of others are valued and expected. Can the president fill such a difficult role? Yes. He can fill it if he is willing to recruit top administrative personnel committed to the same goals and then delegate sufficient authority. The president cannot think of himself as a one man band. He is a conductor maintaining control of the work, but recognizing the importance of solos.

The Junior College Division of the NLHE has developed in-service workshops to prepare education development officers (EDOs). An education development officer assumes the leadership in promoting instructional effectiveness in two-year colleges. He assists the faculty in learning the skills they need to use the systems approach effectively, and he provides them with leadership and technical assistance. He helps the faculty select and state measurable learning objectives by asking two key questions: Is each objective a clear statement of what the student will be able to do after successfully completing a specific task? Do course objectives include a positive attitude toward the subject matter?

The EDO supplies data on student and social needs to help faculty determine course content. The EDO may conduct surveys of student problems, of community employment needs, of skills required for various occupations, and of the academic requirements of the senior institutions. He is not concerned with subject-matter needs; teachers are expected to be experts in their own disciplines. He assists faculty with measurement problems. Here, the EDO raises two key questions: Is the test accompanied by a scoring key or other information which defines adequate performance? Are all test items specifically related to the predetermined learning objectives?

The EDO suggests procedures for item sampling, means of employing data-processing systems, and methods for measuring complex objectives. He also helps establish interinstructor scoring reliability to promote consistency in assessing student achievement.

He helps faculty design appropriate learning activities, and poses several questions about learning activities: Do the activities include frequent practice for the student? Will the student have immediate knowledge of his own progress? Is course content broken into small units, and does each unit consist of learning steps in sequence? Are there provisions for different learning rates? Are directions for the student clear? Are various media employed to allow for different learning styles?

The EDO makes use of his knowledge of learning principles and theories. He makes sure that learning activities are designed to take advantage of psychological findings regarding the learning process. In order to assist teachers in the revision of their learning objectives, activities, and tests, the EDO raises three basic questions: Did the teacher gather all necessary data on student achievement? Did the teacher interview students for added diagnostic data? Did the teacher gather data on student attitudes?

In his own research and evaluation, the EDO observes and describes the total impact of the instructional system at each stage of revision. He also investigates alternative learning activities with the same objectives. A principal function of the EDO is to exploit research methodologies in order to improve instruction. He investigates any factor which he thinks might influence learning and applies the results directly to the program. He also provides data to the college president and others who determine administrative policies, practices, and procedures. Some of these areas are: admissions policies, counseling and placement services, grading practices, and class withdrawal procedures. When the administration makes decisions in learning-related areas, the EDO evaluates their impact on learning. This function is important because the EDO is expected to increase the number of administrative decisions based on research related directly to learning.

EDOs are now furnishing instructional support and leadership for community colleges throughout the nation. But the Educational Development Officer system is applicable to more than just one individual. Educational development includes many functions that can be divided among various college staff members. Some colleges have established education development teams. Team members are drawn from student services, instruction, and administration. However, the focus of the educational development team is on improved instruction—ways to improve student retention and student achievement.

The concept of mastery learning has profound implications for community colleges. All college personnel are affected when a college prepares to develop a viable, efficient learning system—a system that makes it possible for most students who enroll to achieve their educational objectives successfully. Trustees, presidents, and key staff are committed to serving the community that supports the college and to making education meaningful to those segments of the population who need it most desperately.

6

Motivating Teachers

*I*n planning a course, the teacher must analyze the content he wishes to present and the behaviors he wishes to achieve. Burton (1962, pp. 124–132) contends that maintaining a balance between objectives that are too general and those that are too limited is a great difficulty. Bloom's system of classifying cognitive objectives (Bloom and others, 1956) and Krathwohl's taxonomy of affective objectives (Krathwohl and others, 1964) are briefly presented here in order to demonstrate how such systems fit into the suggested philosophical base and how they are consistent with the learning principles mentioned earlier. This presentation focuses our general consideration of mastery learning and the systems approach into a practical set of guidelines which instructors can use to apply our rationale.

Affective objectives may be thought of in terms of the student's attitude toward learning. Did the student like the course? Did he appreciate it? Would he take the course again? Would he recommend it to others? Has he been sufficiently motivated to consider learning an intrinsic self-generating drive?

He must also increase his commitment to such learning. We present the following taxonomies in strict hierarchical order on the assumption that clearly established levels of cognitive and affective performance exist, each building on and extending the abilities of the previous level. This assumption holds true for groups. However, an individual does not necessarily progress through all the steps, nor do all individuals start at the same point in cognitive abilities or motivational "set" (attitude toward learning expected in a given situation). Our discussion of the systems approach indicates that the teacher should formulate his objectives and then assess the student's initial level of competence. The importance of the pre-assessment can be seen in light of this discussion—it tells the teacher and the student where the student is and where instruction should begin. If a preassessment test is carefully constructed and includes items designed to check the student's affective attitudes, the instructor may find he needs to allow additional time to establish his preconditions before jumping into the cognitive meat of the unit.

Each teacher should attempt to develop instruction at all levels of the cognitive hierarchy. Consider the following objective: The learner will, without reference to any aids (notes, text, or another student) list and briefly describe (in a sentence or two) the four major components of the systems approach. What level of cognition is required? To the learner who is not familiar with the systems approach and has simply memorized the four phases and a brief definition of each the objective is a simple recall of information (a knowledge objective). But the same objective may require comprehension if the learner has written a definition of each phase, correct in content, but clearly distinct from the author's definition. Perhaps most behavioral objectives, even when unambiguous, may be measuring different levels of cognition in different learners. The same can be said for affective objectives. For a learner with verbal difficulties, asking a simple question or giving a short verbal answer to a teacher's question may call for a high level of commitment. However, for the student who is verbal and who comes from a home where the parents are educated and spend much time talking with their children and encouraging their opinions, a verbal response to a question or the question itself may be almost automatic and require little commitment.

Affective and cognitive objectives are always related and are separated here only for clarity. A taxonomy helps the reader check his objectives and avoid undue concentration on a single level of learning.

Cognitive Learning

The first level of cognitive learning is knowledge. We use the term to mean ability to remember. Knowledge is analogous to the openness stage of the Mooney model. Perception is its source. The information to be memorized may be simple or complex, concrete or abstract. The development of imagery systems for storing information is important at this stage. For learners with low abilities in abstract learning, extensive use of audio-visual systems (which help to build missing or to correct faulty images) is probably necessary. Once images or memory plans are developed, abstract materials may be increasingly used. All the learner is required to do at this stage is to recall information. This low-level objective is important because later abilities will be limited by the amount and quality of stored information. The stored information should be as meaningful as possible. The most important aspect of knowledge is not quantity of information but economy and power.

The second level of cognitive learning is comprehension. Comprehension probably constitutes the largest class of educational objectives. Included in this class are translation, interpretation, and extrapolation. The comprehension level corresponds to integration in the Mooney model. The learner makes associations between bits of stored information so that meaningful relations are established. Although it is not clear how this process operates, we hypothesize interaction between one's view of the world and his symbolic manipulations. If this theory is correct, students with low abstraction abilities may need considerable audio-visual assistance in order to comprehend abstract systems. Sequence is important to comprehension.

A Modest Proposal: Students Can Learn

If the levels of communication contain gaps or are too hard or too easy, they affect the student's predisposition toward learning.

The third level of cognitive learning is application. Given a problem, the learner applies an abstraction without being told which one to select. The concept of application is important because it embodies the notion of transfer of training. Application corresponds to Mooney's transaction phase—the learner operates on his environment. This stage is also the first test of the learner's generalizing ability. The nature of the problem at this stage must be seen as meaningful and not as just a trumped-up exercise. Problem selection may be difficult because it is a function of the value judgment of the selector. We see an opportunity here for the learner to assist the selector in the planning of topics or problems to be studied. If attention is given to the relative value of problems in helping the student to understand and cope with his environment, the learner develops his own value basis. Incidentally, such a process may also help define (or perhaps transfer from the unconscious to the conscious) the teacher's own value orientations. Formally, in this stage man's tendencies to err (prejudice) may be brought to light and examined.

The fourth stage of cognitive learning is analysis. The learner tries to break down ideas into their component parts in order to discover their relationships. This stage corresponds to the generalized problem-solving level in the Mooney system. It makes use of all the abilities discussed up to this point. The learner tries to analyze his environment so that he may systematically interact with it. The learner first perceives a problem. He then goes to his stored images and looks for similarities. At this point, the process either fails or succeeds, depending upon the extent of information previously stored. If the student finds few similarities, he realizes that he has tackled too difficult a problem and stops. If he finds many similarities, he begins restructuring the problem in terms of his stored information. Once he has classified the problem, he selects a suitable abstraction (for instance, a concept or a theory) and uses it to solve the problem.

We can see why teachers do not attempt to teach at this

level and the two higher ones. Unless one has carefully developed the prior information required to solve this type of problem, the process is likely to be short-circuited in its early stages. If the teacher has not developed behavioral objectives at the lower levels, he is hard pressed to begin at this level. The same exists in the next two categories. If a teacher assigns a problem without initially analyzing the behavioral competence required to solve it, he may conclude that the students are unable to operate at such a level.

The fifth stage of cognitive learning is synthesis. In this stage the learner attempts to put together elements to form a whole—to make a new, clear pattern from an unclear one. This stage corresponds to the creation phase of the Mooney model. The student produces something—something which he can observe and something which is more than was available at the start. This something might be a poem or a story, for instance. Encouraging students to be unique is the key to synthesis. Such teaching demands tolerance of confusion, trial-and-error behavior, and a low-threat atmosphere. The teacher can expect little originality if he judges performance on a group-based scale. The standard must be the individual.

The final stage of cognitive learning is evaluation. In this stage the learner makes judgments about the value of ideas, works, solutions, methods, and so forth. He formulates criteria or standards for appraising the extent to which a particular situation is accurate, effective, economical, or satisfying. This stage (along with the application stage) corresponds to Mooney's transaction phase. However, our cognitive evaluation is on a higher level than is Mooney's transaction phase. The learner must have ordered his environment and have integrated his values with his perceptions in order to compare independently his set of values with external sets. On the basis of these reasoned judgments, he either modifies his values or maintains them intact. Such comparison (and modification) of values is the culmination of the learning process. If the process has been successful, the individual is in control of his intellectual fate. He is able to accept that which is reasonable and reject that which is not. If the process has not been successful, the individual remains dependent upon the ideas of others and is persuaded by whatever seems most compelling at the moment. The individual who has not encountered values before the evaluation stage is influenced by quick opinions and feelings, rather than by considered judgments. We find it frightening that many people, including teachers, fail to distinguish between quick opinions and reasoned judgments.

Affective Learning

Krathwohl and others (1964) noted that the major problem in categorizing the affective domain is the traditional terminology (labels such as attitudes, values, appreciations, and interests). They decided that these labels are too vague and general and should be abandoned. Instead, the authors used the term *process of internalization*—the extent to which one has become committed to a given value or set of values—to describe one's observable behavior. The following stages range from limited commitment (internalization) to actual behavior to total commitment (internalization) which directs a series of related behaviors.

The first stage is receiving. We define this stage as the willingness to become aware of stimuli. This ability is closely related to the cognitive objective of knowledge. Affective receiving, however, does not require that one memorize or recall exactly a given stimulus: he need only be aware of its existence. We can break up receiving into three subcategories: awareness, willingness to receive stimuli, and controlled or selected attention. At no point in this stage need the learner respond to, or become emotionally involved with, the stimuli. We might best describe it as helping the learner become sensitized to the existence of phenomena and stimuli. Learning psychologists tell us that we perceive information selectively, often not realizing we are blocking many perceptions. Cognitive-field theorists report that one's life space (that portion of the environment which is noticed by an individual) is dynamic. Receiving, then, implies developing an awareness of those aspects of his environment which we want him to select. Initially, this awareness is unconscious (such as realizing that a radio is playing in the background). As unawareness gives way, the individual might reach the willingness substage and decide to leave the radio on (tolerate it) rather than turn it off. Finally, he might note (selected attention) that he likes fast songs better than ballads.

The second stage of affective learning is responding. At this level the individual goes beyond receiving and acts or responds to stimuli. The first level might be compared with the process of setting up preconditions for motivation. At the second level, the individual shows his motivation by his actions. This level is subdivided in terms of the nature of the response. First, the individual is simply willing to show his acquiescence in responding, that is, the individual is ready to comply with the rules. Next, he shows willingness to respond. He engages on his own in activities, or he contributes to activity such as a class discussion without being called on. Finally, he demonstrates satisfaction in his response. When a response becomes enjoyable it may also become self-generating (intrinsic). The individual may find he enjoys reading and does so whenever he can, whether or not it is necessary for a class. If the teacher has effectively designed the learning activities and carefully considered motivation, most learners respond at the third level. This level is perhaps most closely related to the integrative stage of the Mooney model. The individual learns to integrate his perceptions with appropriate behavior or actions.

The third stage of affective learning is valuing. We define this level as the ability of the individual to attribute worth to a phenomenon or behavior. This category is based primarily on external rather than internal values. Some social beliefs, values, and products gradually become internalized and accepted by the student as his own. They are consistent and stable enough to be expected in appropriate situations. We can compare valuing with the integration stage of the Mooney model. Valuing represents a higher level of integration than does responding and includes some environmental interactions. At this stage the individual comes to know his environment and begins to structure his values so that they are relatively consistent with those of his society. We can identify three substages in this category: acceptance of a value—the willingness to be perceived by others as having a given value, preference for a value—working or acting in support of a value, and commitment—deep and sustained support of a given value.

The next stage of affective learning is organizing. At this stage, the student manipulates previously internalized values into an order or system which assigns priorities to and determines the interrelationship of one's values. This process is related to the transactional phase of the Mooney model. The individual gains from his environment information which aids him in defining and ordering his values. He then acts on his environment, which may alter the information he receives. The success of his actions aids him further in organizing his internalized values. The conceptualization of a value—finding the basic underlying assumptions, such as a code of ethics—is a prerequisite to this stage.

The final stage of affective learning is characterizing. At this level of internalization, values are already hierarchically ordered and are part of an internally consistent system. Individual behavior has been controlled by ordered value systems for so long that the individual has adopted set ways and need not become emotional over his actions. He is able to operate automatically in a consistently integrated way. He does not have to stop and ask himself why he did something. The task then is to expand such behavior to even wider areas of behavior and to assist the individual to further integrate his value system until it becomes a total philosophy or world view. This level represents the culmination of the Mooney model. The individual is now capable of effective creation, which he uses to understand himself and his environment. The learner becomes an independent operator.

Individualized Instruction

The remainder of this chapter discusses individualized instructional programs (self-instructional units) and the principles of programing. The teacher begins by determining his objectives. He screens his objectives against a philosophical base, the general goals of his subject field, and the needs of individual students. Once he has made these decisions, he determines behavioral goals. He pretests the students to prevent duplication of learning and to assure himself that they have the appropriate prerequisites. Then he designs the learning experiences for each instructional sequence so that the objectives of the sequence are covered, and provision is made for a variety of learning experiences. (No one style of learning should be followed to the exclusion of all others.)

Self-instructional units may lose their effectiveness if they offer only traditional, symbolic sets of readings. True, learning rates would be more flexible, and objectives would be stated in behavioral terms. But the low-abstract learner would still be little encouraged or assisted. We suggest two ways an instructor can provide variety in learning styles in self-instructional units. First, each unit can incorporate a variety of learning activities ranging from straight reading and answering questions to audio-visual aids. These aids must be an integral part of the learning sequence, not afterthoughts tacked on to traditional learning sequences. Second, each learning sequence may be designed in several forms. For example, one sequence might stress reading and another symbolic activities. Such a sequence might be the best means for high abstract-ability learners. Another sequence might feature a series of sound slides, a filmstrip, a taped lecture, or a step-by-step illustrated experiment. This approach might be optimal for low abstract-ability students. The greater the variety, the more closely the teacher approaches optimal learning sequences for all students. The teachers must also test the units on a few sample learners (particularly slow learners) in order to determine whether the terminology is clear before beginning general usage of a sequence.

The final step in the systems approach is evaluation. Evaluation serves two purposes. First, it tells the learner how well he has done in terms of the behavioral objectives of the unit. Second, it provides the instructor with information about the strengths or weaknesses of the unit, so that he may revise his work.

The following pages present a detailed discussion of each of the four basic steps in the systematic approach to instruction. The examples are drawn from units developed by instructors who teach in community colleges, and all examples have been used in community colleges. These examples are not the final word. The reader is urged to be critical in his appraisal and to use these examples as a springboard for devising effective and imaginative sequences of his own.

We have already said a good deal about behavioral objectives. We need reiterate here only that clearly stated objectives provide the direction for all other phases of self-instructional learning. In 1950, Wrinkle (p. 93) made two general observations which are still applicable. He said: "It did not dawn on us until 1938 [that] if the end product of a part of a youngster's experience could and should be measured in terms of what he does, the end product of all educative experience is the modification of behavior of the learner." Sadly, educators have not widely accepted this view. Perhaps the reason, as Wrinkle (p. 98) observes, is "that pencil-and-paper tests are of much less importance than you may have thought and that much greater emphasis will have to be given to the development of means whereby it can be determined whether the student does the things which should result from his experience." Determining behavior implies action on the part of the learner. We need to ask ourselves what learner behaviors demonstrate cognitive and affective performance. We must then phrase our objectives in accordance with such action words.

Cognitive objectives range from simple recall of information to complex evaluations of strategies, systems, and relationships. What actions are called for at each stage? Let us first examine the knowledge phase. The following are typical objectives which test the learner's internalization of simple recall information.

(1) The learner will list Terman's factors that are most predictive of a successful marriage.

(2) The learner will memorize Sturk and Johnson's definition of the psychology of religion.

(3) The learner will recall the names of the fifty states.

(4) The learner will correctly match a list of presidential policy statements given in his text with the correct president.

(5) The learner will correctly state Boyle's Law.

(6) Given the names of three contemporary composers, the learner shall give the name of one composition by each.

The following objectives are designed to test comprehension.

(1) Given English forms of greeting, the student shall give the appropriate French equivalent, but not an exact translation.

(2) The learner will in his own words explain the law of supply and demand.

(3) The student will explain the meaning of a graph illustrating population trends.

(4) After reading a list of sentences, the learner will decide which ones would make good topic sentences.

(5) Given a series of graphs, the learner will select the graph which best illustrates Newton's law of gravity expressed by the formula $F = G\ (m_1\ m_2/d^2)$.

(6) Given a list of statements concerning planning a family budget, the learner will mark true or false beside each statement and will then correct the false statements so that they become true statements.

The following questions are designed to test application.

(1) The learner shall convincingly represent a member of a taxpayer's association during a mock meeting of the city council.

(2) Given a blueprint of a dog house, the learner will build a dog house exactly as shown by the blueprint.

(3) The learner will conduct an experiment with another learner to prove the existence of emotion.

(4) Given a variety of foods and using his knowledge of the effects of heat and air on food preservation, the learner will store the given foods so they will be edible at the end of one week.

The next three stages of cognitive learning—analysis, synthesis, and evaluation—are not often employed, probably because they are time-consuming and their objectives are difficult to state in behavioral terms. The following are analysis objectives.

(1) The learner will state Jung's view of religion and compare it with Freud's.

(2) Given a list of twenty brief arguments, the learner will

correctly identify seventeen fallacies in the reasoning and decide which of the four types of fallacies in reasoning are *argumentum ad hominem, post hoc* fallacy, false analogy, and hasty generalization.

(3) Given a series of unknown chemicals and using any tests he wishes, the learner will identify each of the chemicals. He may use any aids he wishes and has four laboratory periods in which to complete this task. He must work alone.

(4) Given a tape recorded description of an automobile accident, the learner will write a capsule summary of the accident suitable for a news release and including the following points: who, what, when, where, how, and why (this is interpreted as the *single major reason* for the accident). The learner may use only the tape and may not write more than a one-page story.

The following are synthesis objectives.

(1) The learner will write a brief (not more than five pages) history of how psychology has approached religion from Wundt to the present. Any reference materials may be employed.

(2) The learner will prepare for delivery to a local Rotary Club a speech entitled "Why the Two-Year College Is the Best Avenue for the Lower-Ability College-Age Youths in Our Country." This speech will be a twenty- to thirty-minute speech and should be easily understood by people who are generally uninformed about two-year colleges.

(3) Given a list of fixed conditions such as the cost of materials, building specifications, purposes, and money available, the learner will prepare a plan for a new community recreation center. The student may use any available plans as guides but must stay within the available funds and meet at least 75 per cent of the stated purposes of the recreation center.

The following are evaluation objectives.

(1) Given a list of six criteria (the six most frequently selected types of sites for new settlements, such as fall line, sheltered harbor, mountain pass, fertile river valley, mouth of a major river, etc.) the learner will select from a series of maps of possible site locations the most likely location for a settlement.

(2) Given a tentative research project, the learner will write

a critique of the design according to Campbell and Stanley's criteria for research designs.

(3) The learner will listen to a symphony written by a contemporary composer. He will then write a review of the performance based on his own criteria, which are to be stated at the start of his review.

(4) Given the statement "Negroids are biologically inferior to Caucasoids," the learner will evaluate this statement in terms of the most generally accepted anthropological position.

The foregoing examples might well have been extended to more clearly specify the precise materials to be manipulated, conditions under which they would be met, and the specific criterion for completion. The example in Table 3 of a fully elaborated general

Table 3. FOUNDATIONS ENGLISH OBJECTIVES

Students are placed in Foundations English in accordance with the student's performance on standard tests. The following objectives indicate the level of performance required of the student before entrance into:

English 101, which is required for most two-year programs.

Freshman English 111, which is required for students who wish to transfer to a four-year school.

Objectives for 101:

I. The student must be able to demonstrate ability to perform consistently by meeting the following objectives in at least three papers. The third paper must be written on a topic announced at the beginning of a class period, and it must be completed within sixty minutes.

1. These papers must consist of at least three paragraphs:
   A. An introductory statement of thirty to fifty words, without a topic sentence, with a thesis sentence near the end.
   B. A middle paragraph(s) of forty-five to one hundred words, with a topic sentence which is near the beginning, with detail supporting the thesis. If two paragraphs are written, both must be seventy-five to one hundred words, with a topic sentence.
   C. A concluding statement of thirty to fifty words (without a topic sentence) which develops a logical conclusion based

97

on the middle paragraph or which summarizes the prior material.

II. Any one of the following fallacies in logic will disqualify a paper.

1. *Hasty Generalization.* Example: If a train has been late twice, we may not generalize that the railroad never runs on time. That would be a generalization based on inadequate evidence.

2. *Post hoc ergo propter hoc* (after this, therefore because of this). Example: "I washed and polished my car and it rained; therefore, washing and polishing my car caused it to rain."

3. *Appeal to an Unqualified Authority.* Example: "We should eat Cereal X because Mickey Mantle says it is best." Mantle is qualified to talk expertly about baseball, but he is not qualified by training or experience to give an expert opinion on nutrition.

4. *False Analogy.* Reasoning by analogy is a legitimate process; however, it can distort and mislead if employed improperly. Example: "Democrats believe in public ownership of some utilities; so do Communists and Socialists; therefore: Democrats are Communists."

5. *Polar Thinking.* Polar thinking is usually expressed by the terms *either* and *or*. Example: "You are either with us or against us. If you are a good American, you will vote Democratic." In polar thinking no alternative is permitted.

6. *Argumentum ad hominem* (attacking the person). Example: "We cannot listen to the opposition. He is a misfit, an agitator, and complainer."

7. *"God" and "Devil" words* (slanted language). Many words are open to personal definition. They are loaded with emotional implications, and the writer should be careful to define words loaded with emotional content: patriot, Old Glory, socialism, propaganda, Christian, radical, conservative, liberal, fascist, free enterprise, communism, etc.

8. *Circular Reasoning.* Example: "Virginia is the greatest state in the union because I've lived here all my life." Another example: "It's the right thing to do because it's the right action to take." Another example: "This is a good theme because I know what a good theme is."

9. *Unqualified Statement.* An unqualified statement is a statement that is not true because too many categories are included in the statement. "Everybody enjoys Christmas" is an unqualified statement. It is not true because some people don't enjoy Christmas. The statement can be qualified by saying, "Almost everyone enjoys Christmas," or "Most people enjoy Christmas."

III. The following words and phrases may not be used in any context:

in today's world	I think
in this modern day and age	in my opinion
in the world of today	you
in conclusion	your
to me	good
generation of today	bad
today's generation	really
	very
	just
	great
	fantastic

IV. The following number and types of errors per paper will be allowed:

Spelling 2	Subject-Verb Agreement 2
Punctuation 4	Parallelism 2
Fragments 0	Pronoun-Reference Agreement 2
Run-On Sentences 0	Tense Shift 1
Comma Splice 0	Shift in Point of View 1
Awkward Sentence 1	Wrong Word 2
Contractions 0	Word Needed
	Meaningless Sentence 0

V. In addition, the student must show an ability to use a variety of sentence patterns. The papers should include at least two compound sentences and two complex sentences, as well as simple sentences. It should be noted that any breach of standard English is allowable, provided the student has indicated on his paper that he is aware of the breach and has employed it as a writing technique. However, statements may not be repeated verbatim, except for reasons stated above.

Objectives for 111:

I. All objectives stated in sections I, II, III, and V are applicable to students who aspire to enter English 111.

II. The following number and types of errors per paper will be allowed:

Spelling 1	Subject-Verb Agreement 1
Punctuation 2	Parallelism 1
Fragments 0	Pronoun-Reference Agreement 1

A Modest Proposal: Students Can Learn

Run-On Sentences 0	Tense Shift 0
Comma Splice 0	Shift in Point of View 0
Awkward Sentence 1	Wrong Word 0
Contractions 0	Word Needed 0
	Meaningless Sentence 0

(large scale) objective for a basic English course illustrates how one might translate a general goal such as "the student will demonstrate effective writing" into a completely elaborated behaviorally stated objective.

In this section we present several affective objectives ranging from low to high learner commitment. Action words are the key. The instructor must decide what behavior demonstrates a particular affective state. The following are low-level objectives because they require little internalization of values.

(1) Learners shall read a newspaper editorial on freedom of speech when assigned as homework.

(2) Learners will listen to what is said during a class discussion on freedom of speech.

The following objectives require response and some internalization of values. They also show that one may have to measure outcomes outside the course framework.

(1) The learner will read editorials in the local paper and voluntarily point out weaknesses in the editorials in class.

(2) The learner will suggest topics for class consideration or for additional self-instructional units.

(3) The learner will express in a group discussion his reactions to a field trip to a mental hospital.

(4) The learner will express in a group discussion his personal views on the double standard and premarital sex.

(5) The learner will check out from the school library additional, nonrequired books on machine operation.

(6) The learner, after completing a beginning swimming class, will decide to join the YMCA advanced swim classes.

(7) During the following school year, the learner will enroll for additional English courses which are not required.

(8) The learner will vote in the next election if he is of age.

The next group of objectives requires high degrees of personal commitment to developed value systems.

(1) The learner will defend a student who dropped out of school to work when he hears others criticize the former student unfairly.

(2) The learner will defend a fellow student's right to advocate governmental censorship of news.

(3) The learner will refuse to smoke marijuana even though his peer group gives him a "hard time."

(4) The learner will consistently refuse to say bad things of others or to repeat "gossip."

(5) The learner will finish college even though he is urged by his family to "go to work."

Pretest

We find it difficult to present examples of representative pretests because of the variety of self-instructional units. The primary purpose of a pretest, as we suggested earlier, is to allow the teacher to assess the initial abilities of his students against the expected behavioral outcomes. Two requirements must be provided for in a pretest. First, the pretest must provide a complete cross section of the behaviors required by individual learners (as stated in the unit's objectives). Second, the pretest should attempt to define (in terms of student responses to the test items) what kinds of learning deficiencies are present. This last point is especially crucial and seldom adequately observed in pretests. Learners with low abstraction abilities may show little previous knowledge of unit objectives on a typical abstract pretest. Yet, the concepts, if put into informal terms, may well be understood. The teacher should attempt to design pretests in such a way as to examine as many kinds of learning as possible, in addition to content. After all, the primary purpose of a pretest is to gather information which is helpful to the teacher in revising or implementing his unit, not to obtain a measure against which to gauge later grades (although this can also be done if desired).

How does one design such pretests? Unfortunately, little con-

A Modest Proposal: Students Can Learn

crete information is available. However, a teacher can ask himself whether his pretest is evaluating a learner's vocabulary (special terminology) rather than the concepts he intends to teach. If the answer is yes, then he should modify the pretest questions by eliminating confusing terminology. Terminology should be used only if it is in itself part of the behavioral objectives. Our first example (Table 4) is a typical pretest. It closely parallels the eight objectives

Table 4. SEX PRETEST

1. In the space allowed, place the letter of the stage of sexual development described by the following statements:

    ....1. child learns proper sex identification   A. self-love

    ....2. child learns to respect self   B. parent-identification

    ....3. boys criticize girls   C. gang stage

    ....4. girls control the game of "sex, not-sex"   D. American Dating Game

2. List four *wrong* motives for sex

    A. ....

    B. ....

    C. ....

    D. ....

3. State the four views toward sex Hiltner mentions and indicate which seems to be most psychologically sound.

    1. ....

    2. ....

    3. ....

    4. ....

4. Indicate which of the following statements refer to "TA" (Total

102

Abstinence), "DS" (Double Standard), or P/A (Permissiveness with Affection) as views toward premarital sex.

☐ 1. OK for males, wrong for females before marriage

☐ 2. If two people genuinely love each other, then sex is right before marriage

☐ 3. Sex for sex's sake

☐ 4. Always wrong under any conditions

5. List the first five factors that Lewis Terman considers most predictive of marital happiness and discuss why they are more important than sex.

A. ....

B. ....

C. ....

D. ....

E. ....

6. Write a brief reaction to Frederick Wood's chapel speech, "Sex Within the Created Order." [Taped.] [Space for answer.]

7. Express views on (1) premarital sex and (2) double standard to group. [Space for answer.]

OBJECTIVES

Learner will:

(1) write a brief history of sexual development;

(2) analyze wrong motives for sex;

(3) list and describe Hiltner's four views of sex;

(4) evaluate Bell's thesis about premarital sex;

(5) explain psychological effects of premarital sex;

(6) list Terman's factors that are most predictive of a successful marriage;

(7) write a reaction to the taped chapel speech on "Sex Within the Created Order";

(8) express personal views on the double standard and premarital sex to your group.

of the self-instructional unit. The objectives are given at the end of the pretest in order to allow the reader to compare the two. Normally, the objectives would be included later in a separate section of the unit.

Item 1 tests objective 1. Items 2 and 3 test objectives 2 and 3. Item 4 checks (without mentioning Bell) whether the student is familiar with Bell as required in objective 4. Items 5 through 7 correspond to objectives 6 through 8. Only objective 5 was not directly sampled on the pretest because of its similarity to objectives 4 and 5. The pretest enables the teacher to check the student's content knowledge and his affective reactions (items 6 and 7). The instructor may also get a sample of a student's writing ability. Evaluation of each student's responses should point out learning deficiencies in organization skills and his willingness to submit personal feelings to others in writing. Clearly, the last two items on this pretest make it a potential source of unit revision (feedback on objectives).

Table 5 is two pretests in one. The first part calls for defini-

Table 5.   LATITUDE, LONGITUDE, AND MAP DISTORTION

(Pretest)

1. Define the following terms:
   A. Grid
   B. Latitude
   C. Longitude
   D. Distortion in maps of the world

2. You and a friend have two sheets of plain paper the same size. You place a mark on your piece of paper. *Without showing your paper to your friend* tell him exactly where the mark is so that he can put a mark in the same spot on his paper. When you put the two pieces of paper on top of each other, the marks should fall on top of each other. You cannot place your mark on the corner of the paper and you cannot use a ruler or other measuring aid.

104

3. You are in a power boat (twenty-five-foot inboard) belonging to your friend and there is no land in sight. You hit a floating log and begin to sink. Your friend has a chart of the area [map]. He puts a mark on the chart and starts to call for help. Before he gets anyone on the radio he slips and is knocked out. Using his mark on the chart, explain how you would give your location.

4. You notice that the world map in the front of your classroom pictures Greenland as being as large as the United States. You look up Greenland in your geography book and find that it is quite small (not even one-fourth as large as the United States). Why does it look so big on the map?

tions of the terms elaborated in the unit objectives. If the learner proves on the test that he knows these terms, he need not do the unit. A failure in the first part, however, may indicate only that the student is unfamiliar with the terms. Consequently, the remainder of the pretest items are situational questions designed to measure the student's understanding of the concepts without confusing him with the formal terms. This approach also allows the teacher to measure his learner's capability for forming images.

Learning Activities

The range of learning activities is limited only by the instructor's imagination and the availability (in terms of time and cost) of needed materials. The full range of learning activities can only be hinted at here. L. Johnson (1969) presents the full range of activities that are being used in various two-year colleges. Johnson organizes his examples into categories such as audio-tutorial techniques, programed materials, and independent study. Individualized instruction is not limited to paperwork.

Behavioral objectives of the pretest:

Objective 1:   The student will be able to tell another student by means of a grid system exactly where he has placed a mark on a piece of paper by conducting a two-person exercise and using only two pieces of unlined paper of the same size.

Objective 2:   The student will be able to show how a system of vertical and horizontal lines can be used to locate an object's position.

Objective 3: The student will be able to demonstrate to another student, using a concrete object (such as an orange), why a true picture of the world cannot be shown accurately on a flat surface.

Equally important, any behavior change which can be specifically stated may be analyzed and supported with appropriate learning activities. The instruction unit is a means of directing learning activities, not an end in itself. Learning activities need not be self-contained. Group sessions, for instance, may be built into the unit. Self-instructional units do not automatically depersonalize instruction. Teachers exposed to self-instruction for the first time usually object to the procedure on emotional grounds. They argue that no package can replace the close personal contact of the teacher. A unit as we define it might program in such a relationship. Also, for many learners, close personal contact is not always perceived as positive. Too often, close personal contact is reserved for the best or the worst students. The good student will probably learn under any method. For the bad student, however, the contact may be negative and may inhibit learning. The middle group is often largely ignored. A carefully designed self-instructional unit provides features which personal teaching cannot. Objectives are clear, the activities are directly related to the accomplishment of the objectives, and the learner is constantly provided with feedback against which he can evaluate his success. Furthermore, the teacher is free to see students on an individual basis when they need help.

Self-instructional units can be meaningless, however, if the unit is simply an abbreviated, carefully programed text. If the learning activities are all based on readings in various texts and are followed by questions to be answered, the instructor has done nothing more than systematize traditional instruction. A good self-instruction unit goes beyond texts. Any media may be incorporated into the unit, provided that they directly and clearly relate to a desired behavioral goal. For example, the teacher might require the student to visit a mental hospital and report on his reactions in a small group session. The student might be directed to a sound-on-slide series illustrating an experiment. The student might be asked to conduct an opinion poll of his fellow students on a particular topic or question. The student might be directed to a movie or a tape. The student might be asked to prepare a brief talk to be given at a later full-class session. The student might be asked to tutor a group of slower students.

Tables 6 through 11 illustrate some possible learning activities. The reader is urged to develop his own "list." The examples are taken from units developed by Richard Morgan, psychology professor at Mitchell College in Statesville, North Carolina.* Although the examples are limited to one subject, Morgan is not using his units simply as an effective means of programing cognitive objectives. He uses a wide range of learning activities.

Table 6 shows how a unit may condense text material and

Table 6. FREUDIAN COMPLEXES

THE PHALLIC STAGE

It is important to realize that these experiences which Freud describes took place mainly in the unconscious mind of the child. There are two terms Freud used to describe these experiences: *the oedipus complex for the boy, and the electra complex for the girl.*

1. The Oedipus Complex
The little boy falls in love with his mother but is aware of his father as a rival. He realizes that his father and mother go to bed together, but he has to sleep alone. He actually wishes his father would die, so he could have his mother all to himself. Although he hates his father, he is *afraid* of him. Why? Not only because his father is bigger and stronger, but because he is afraid his father will cut off his penis. Freud called this "castration anxiety." Realizing that he cannot lick his father, the little boy decides to join him. He resolves the complex by identifying with his father, hoping that some day he will find another woman

---

* Reprinted with permission of the publisher. From *Psychology: An Individualized Course,* by Richard L. Morgan. Copyright © 1970 by Westinghouse Learning Corporation.

to love like his mother. Now, let's diagram the Oedipal complex to make it clearer:

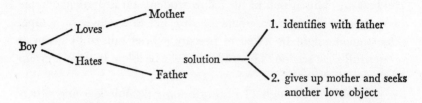

The Oedipal complex takes place in the boy who is in love with his mother and both hates his father as a rival and yet fears him because of his castration anxiety. He identifies with his father and gives up his mother as his love object.

Check the following statements (X) which describe the Oedipus complex.

...............1. Boy hates his father as his rival

...............2. Girl hates her mother

...............3. Boy is afraid mother will castrate him

...............4. Boy identifies with father to overcome fears

...............5. Boy loves his father as a sex object

You should have checked only 1, 4.

Source: Morgan, 1970.

present the essential ideas in a brief learning activity followed by a brief test to reenforce the learning and inform the learner of his progress.

The unit in Table 7, in part, combines a series of slides with

Table 7. HARLOW'S MONKEY EXPERIMENT

Go to the A-V LAB, library room L1, and ask for *Psychology Slides* #17–27. These slides describe Professor Harlow's experiments on "Love in Infant Monkeys," 1958. Some of Harlow's baby monkeys were raised with surrogate (substitute) mothers in their cages. The first was made of wire, hard to the touch, and the second was of foam covered with soft cloth. The wire mother was the source of food for one group of these monkeys. Nursing bottles were built into the center of the wire

mother's chest with nipples protruding. To nurse, the baby monkeys had to climb onto the front. When not eating, they spent most of their time with the cloth mother, clinging to her with all four legs. Gradually, the monkeys spent most of their time with the *cloth mother*. Harlow showed that when the baby monkeys are offered them, they preferred the cloth mother. When confronted with a frightening stimulus, the monkeys fled to the cloth mother. His experiment proved that the need for contact comfort is an innate drive.

Look at Slide 17. Write in the space below what you see:

....

....

I am sure you saw the two surrogate mothers, one made of wire and one of cloth. Both mothers can supply nourishment.

Look at Slide 18. What do you see in this slide? ....
.... Yes, the baby feeds from the wire mother, but still clings to the cloth mother.

Source: Morgan, 1970.

a narrative description of the slides. The learner is approached on the imagerial and the symbolic levels. This learning activity is a good example of how visual media may be integrated into a learning sequence.

Table 8 demonstrates expanded use of audio-visual material.

Table 8. THEORIES OF LEARNING

It is important to know theories of learning because they explain *why* and *how* learning has taken place. Go to the AV LAB in the Library, ask for *Psychology slides* 15 and 16 and *Psychology Tape,* Program #2.

Source: Morgan, 1970.

The answers are provided on the tape. The learner is reenforced and stimulated visually, aurally, and symbolically.

Tables 9 through 11 show how group and individual con-

A Modest Proposal: Students Can Learn

Table 9. ATTITUDES OF BLACKS

You have just learned Eric Lincoln's thesis that there are three groups of black people in our culture. In order for you to understand how black people feel in this community and discover which, if any, of these groups are to be found in Statesville, *conduct the following experiment.*

    I. Go to any "Negro janitor, maid, or kitchen helper" and ask them how they feel about interracial matters in Statesville. Ask them about their feelings toward the white people.

    II. Find a black young person at the high school, or anywhere, and ask him the same questions.

    III. See if you can find a "middle-class Negro," i.e., black people who are teachers or employed in local businesses. Unfortunately, you will have difficulty finding such people. This in itself will be a learning experience.

In the space below, write up your findings. This will be of utmost importance for your group discussions; if you want to devise a questionnaire and make this study more "sophisticated," go to it.

Source: Morgan, 1970.

Table 10. GINOTT'S PSYCHOLOGY

Test your learning by applying Ginott's psychology to a living situation involving a child: Observe a child of one to eight in some life situation (anger, fear, disappointment, hostility at parents, sibling rivalry, etc.) and use some of Ginott's phychology. *Write the results of your observation in the space below.* This is part of your posttest and the results will be discussed in an interview with Dr. Morgan.

Source: Morgan, 1970.

Table 11. HEALTH CENTER OBSERVATION

When ten learners have finished the package to this point, you will go in a group and observe the local Iredell County Community mental Health Center. *When you return, write your observations in the space below.*

Source: Morgan, 1970.

110

ferences may be incorporated into units. They also illustrate that learning activities need not be restricted to the formal class group.

Table 9 was taken from a unit entitled "Black Is Beautiful????" Clearly, learners are not restricted to the formal class setting. Also, this learning activity is as much an affective learning exercise as a cognitive exercise. The exercise provides the learner with an opportunity to do some independent thinking about the topic or to design an alternative research program which he will have a chance to test.

Table 10 again shows that the learner can be directed to a larger laboratory to test formal learnings. The exercise also shows that a direct teacher-student conference can be made a part of learning experiences.

Table 11 again shows how a group session may be programed into a learning sequence. It also directs people to go to the larger laboratory, as did Table 10.

Posttest

The posttest is based on the same criteria as the pretest. Both tests must clearly and directly sample the behaviors called for in the unit objectives. This observation may sound trite or obvious. However, teachers who have spent sixteen or twenty years under a traditional system may find it hard to swallow. Much present testing, especially in higher education, is a guessing game in which the students try to anticipate the exam questions. In the mastery system elaborated earlier, the learner knows what questions to expect from the instructor because the questions are extensions of the initial objectives. The purpose of a posttest is to provide the learner with an evaluation of his progress and to provide the teacher with information on the success of the unit so that he may improve it.

In addition to testing the cognitive factors which we discussed earlier (in the pretest examples), the instructor may want to test the attitudinal impact of his unit on the student. The two examples in Tables 12 and 13 illustrate how the teacher might

A Modest Proposal: Students Can Learn

Table 12. REVISION-DATA FORM

1. Give your assessment of the reading(s). [This could be expanded to include all media.]

2. Were the questions clear?............If not, which question(s) gave you the most difficulty? Which should be omitted? Which should be revised? [This question could also refer to any media.]

   3. How much did you enjoy working thru this unit?
   .... very much   .... some   .... very little
   .... none
   Comment:

4. Indicate your perception of the degree to which you "learned" about the topic dealt with in this unit as a result of working thru it.
   .... very much   .... some   .... very little
   .... nothing

5. Which statements best describe your feelings about your involvement with this self-instructional unit.

.... too easy	.... boring
.... inspiring	.... can take it or leave it
.... a waste of time	.... a real treat
.... interesting	.... dull
.... ok	.... too time consuming
.... just another course requirement	.... did it to please the instructor
.... sure beats the traditional approach to education	

6. Indicate the classroom approach you prefer in dealing with this topic of the course:
   .... lecture
   .... outside reading by all followed by class discussion
   .... self-instructional unit during/in place of class time
   .... student reports followed by class discussion
   .... other (please specify) ....

7. Do you feel the material dealt with in this unit is relevant to your present or future needs? Yes............   No............

8. Please state the ways in which this self-instructional unit might be improved.

   Source: B. R. Herrscher.

Table 13. Unit Evaluation Form

1. Was this unit of benefit to you? How?

2. How has your attitude toward the systems approach shifted as a result of this unit? (Circle the appropriate number on the scale.)

−2	−1	0	1	2
Much more Negative	Slightly More Negative	Same	Slightly More Positive	Much More Positive

3. Has your attitude towards self-instruction shifted as a result of this unit? (Circle the appropriate number on the scale.)

−2	−1	0	1	2
Much more Negative	Slightly More Negative	Same	Slightly More Positive	Much More Positive

4. Are there any suggestions you have to make this unit more effective next time? (facilities, equipment and resources available, time schedule, etc.)

measure a learner's affective reactions. Such evaluations must be anonymous, and the student must believe that his comments are in no way a part of his grade. He must also believe that the comments are desired and potentially useful and that the instructor will incorporate the suggestions into revisions of the unit.

Table 13 has been used to evaluate workshops for junior-college teachers. We have substituted the term *unit* for the term *workshop*. We feel that this change in no way alters the value of the instrument. This form makes a more careful attempt to assess the direction and degree of attitude change than did the form in Table 12.

The attitude measures explored in Tables 12 and 13 are not the only ones nor are they necessarily the best possibilities—though they have proven their value. We suggest, however, that some measure of attitude or affective impact be included in every learning unit. The reader is urged to develop and refine his own model. The

113

self-instructional unit is a system for assuring that all elements in a learning sequence are considered. Exactly how these elements are incorporated into the unit is a function of the skill and imagination of the teacher. A self-instructional unit will not transform poor teaching or irrelevant objectives into good teaching and relevant objectives even though it may clarify the steps in the process. In the final analysis, each teacher answers for his own values or lack of values. He must be able to differentiate between the relevant and the irrelevant, the necessary and the digressive, and the interesting and the dull. He must constantly use his experiences to discover how others learn best and incorporate such understanding into his teaching. Perhaps the single most important advantage of our approach is that it furnishes the teacher with feedback.

Table 14 is a miniunit which incorporates all the components of the systems approach described in this chapter. Again, the reader is cautioned to consider such a miniunit only one of many possible approaches.

Some readers may comment that the educational program presented here by us sounds fine; but does it work? Yes, it works. Many colleges and hundreds of instructors have implemented most, if not all, of the ideas developed in this work. Moraine Valley Community College in Palos Hills, Illinois, is an example. In an effort to combat overdepartmentalization and specialization, Moraine Valley operates without individual departments or divisions. Curricular offerings at the college are interrelated, and all faculty members are on an interdisciplinary-curriculum team. The college is built without individual offices in the belief that offices segregate faculty members from each other and from the students. All members of the college, faculty, students, and staff use available space in an open setting. The college also has few interior walls.

The choice of a curriculum is also open and flexible at Moraine Valley. Students may choose from a variety of instructional strategies in order to arrive at behaviorally stated objectives. Instruction is developed to accommodate individual learning rates and to permit learner control of the environment. The president, Robert

Table 14. Bacteria Reproduction

Objectives:

Model of expected performance (oral and printed mediums). Students have list of objectives plus hear them on the tape ⟶

1. Define fission. (*principle learning*) ⟶ Types of learning identified

2. Diagram and label the five steps in bacterial division (*principle learning*) ⟶ Types of learning identified

3. Given the number of bacteria present at a certain time, compute the number that will be present at some time interval hence. (ex. six hours later; one and a half hours later) (*problem solving*) ⟶ Types of learning identified

Learning Activities:

Presenting the stimulus (moving picture) ⟶ *This is a bacterial cell dividing.* This type of multiplication of cells by dividing is called fission. Let's look at this process more closely.

Presenting the stimulus (still picture—diagram) *Here is a young bacterial cell.* It grows to full length (elongates)—at this stage it is called a mature cell. Then division

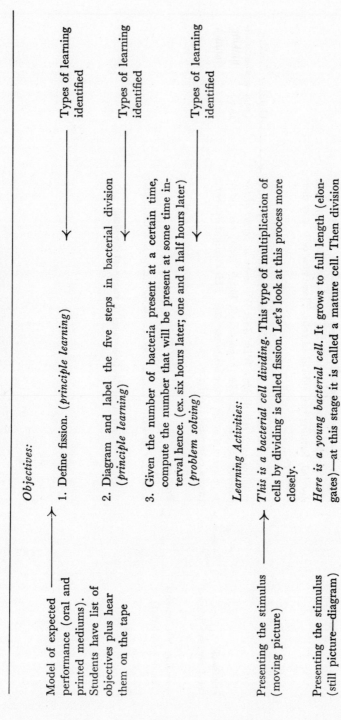

Directing attention ——→
(oral communication)

begins. *Note* how the cell appears to pinch in in the center. This pinching continues until the two halves are completely divided, forming two individual cells. These new cells may then separate.

Feedback ——→
(oral communication)

How fast do bacteria divide? On the average of every thirty minutes each cell divides. *What does this mean in terms of the number in the bacterial population?* That's right, *the entire population doubles every thirty minutes! This constant doubling* causes extremely rapid growth. ↙ —— Guiding thinking (oral communication)

Assessing attainments ——→
(printed material)

Posttest:

1. Define fission: _____

2. Diagram and label the five stages of bacterial division:

    1.

    2.

    3.

    4.

    5.

3. Given that one hundred bacteria are present, how many would be present at the time periods later:

    a) one hour

    b) two and a half hours

Answers:

1. reproduction by dividing into two parts, each of which grows into a complete organism

2. young cell

    mature cell

    division begins

    division completed

    new cells

3. a) 400 cells   b) 3200 cells

Feedback
(printed material)

Source: Washburn, 1971.

Turner, feels that the community college has the obligation to tailor instruction to the needs of the learners who enroll. He feels that Moraine Valley is on target.

Another community college operating on similar principles is Brookdale Community College in Lincroft, New Jersey. The president, Ervin Harlacher, has follow-up data on the success of his students. In its first year of operation, Brookdale had a 90 per cent retention rate. Ninety per cent of all the students who enrolled for the first time in September completed the school year—an unheard-of statistic in community colleges. In fact, we know of few four-year colleges or universities that can boast of a 90 per cent retention rate. Obviously, all the students at Brookdale did not earn the same amount of credit—but they persisted. They stayed in school and moved forward until they realized their educational objectives. If students do not persist, they cannot attain anybody's objectives.

Central Piedmont Community College in Charlotte, North Carolina, is also implementing the concepts of individualized learning through the systems approach. Central Piedmont has developed individualized courses ranging from automobile mechanics to English grammar and composition. Statistics have been kept on the learning success of the students in these courses. Without exception, students persist longer, achieve more, and indicate that they prefer this approach of instruction to any other method they have experienced.

Mitchell College, an independent community college in Statesville, North Carolina, is another two-year college committed to the instructional concepts we have outlined. The general objectives of the program at Mitchell focus specifically on the purpose and techniques of effective teaching. Teaching is a process of causing learning; if no learning occurs, it may be inferred that no teaching has taken place. All faculty and administrators at Mitchell are committed to student learning as the primary goal of the college. Individualized instruction (within the framework of systematic learning) is the basic strategy of the instructional program. Available research on student learning at Mitchell College indicates that the students persist longer and achieve more since the introduction of relevant instructional strategies than they did before. The attrition rate has been reduced at Mitchell, and the students indicate a strong preference for the systematic approach of instruction.

Kittrell Junior College in Kittrell, North Carolina, is another two-year college totally committed to educational accountability by means of systematic instruction. Kittrell (predominantly black) has documented great success with individualized instruction. The board of trustees and Kittrell's president, Larnie Horton, are committed to individualized instruction as a means of accommodating the majority of the students who enroll at Kittrell.

Other colleges that are well on their way to implementing the instructional concepts advocated here include Southeastern Community College in Whiteville, North Carolina; Piedmont Technical Institute in Roxboro, North Carolina; Greenville Technical Institute in Greenville, South Carolina; Wayne Community College in Goldsboro, North Carolina; College of the Mainland, Texas City, Texas; Tarrant County Community College District, Fort Worth; El Centro Community College, Dallas; and Golden West Community College in Huntington Beach, California. These colleges are all moving toward full implementation of systematic instructional strategies. Aside from these institutional endeavors, individual teachers in community colleges throughout the nation have implemented individualized approaches or are in the process of doing so. Traditional methods of classroom instruction have not served the community college population for which they were intended. Nontraditional students require nontraditional instructional approaches. (For that matter, even traditional students would profit from nontraditional approaches.) Evidence from colleges around the country indicates that colleges and students perform best when individual instruction is developed to accommodate individual learning styles and individual student needs.

119

A

Sample Employment Contract

Date ....

Appointee ....

Address ....

Position .... Salary ....

Period of Service ....

College .... Campus ....

Schedule of Payment ....

(twenty or twenty-four installments at option of appointee)

Special Provisions:

    The provisions for benefits to the appointee and obligations and responsibilities from the appointee with which the appointee is charged and agrees to faithfully perform are attached hereto and made a part hereof, and the appointee accepts all of the provisions therein and agrees to comply with all of the requirements therein set forth, all of which benefits and requirements are made a part of this contract as though fully set forth herein.

Appendix A

Please indicate your acceptance by signing and returning the attached copy of this memorandum to the Office of the President on or before

....

....
Accepted and Signed: President

                                                    ....
                                                    Dated: ....

Addenda to the Contract

All of the provisions hereinafter set forth apply to all appointees in their particular position which is set forth on page 1 of this contract and the appointee shall be required to fulfill all of the obligations, requirements, and responsibilities set forth in the section following the title of his or her particular position or as assigned by the president.

SECTION I. GENERAL REQUIREMENTS

A. This contract shall run for a period of .... college years.

   During the term of the contract the faculty members shall:

   (1) Design appropriate plans of learning experiences for at least one course each semester.

   (2) Have these plans approved by the dean of the college based on:

      (a) Behavioral objectives

      (b) Self-instructional and other techniques

      (c) Evaluation procedures

      (d) Available resources

   (3) Implement, manage, and evaluate the learning experiences for the students assigned to your approved courses.

B. The college year consists of the following terms:

   Summer: Six weeks (employment with the college optional)
   Fall: Eighteen weeks
   Winter: Four weeks
   Spring: Eighteen weeks
   Total: Forty-six weeks

C. The basic contract covers forty weeks of instructional responsibility; namely, the fall, winter and spring terms.

D. The faculty members will be limited to teaching one course during the winter term.

E. The faculty member will be expected to teach evenings or at extension centers as part of his regular instructional responsibilities at no extra compensation.

F. The faculty member will devote his entire time and attention to his duties and the position to which he has been appointed, and he will engage in no other business or gainful employment except with the written consent of the president.

G. Renewal of this initial contract shall be at the option of the Passaic County College Board of Trustees upon recommendation of the president.

H. All changes in rank during the term of any contract following the initial contract shall be after notice in writing to the appointee, upon his written application, and upon a hearing before the Passaic County College Board of Trustees.

I. During the period of this contract, the faculty member shall successfully complete, at college expense, one graduate course per semester as scheduled in the following areas:
   (1) Philosophy of community-junior colleges.
   (2) Writing and classification of behavioral objectives.
   (3) Self-instructional techniques and methods.
   (4) Multimedia materials and methods.
   (5) Evaluation procedures for self-paced instruction, both formative and summative.

SECTION II. AREA OF RESPONSIBILITY

A. The initial pretenure period of which this contract covers the first year, is one of learning new skills, attitudes, and sensitivities, and will include minimal institutional governance responsibilities. This will be necessary because of the extraordinary responsibilities outlined in Section I, Paragraphs A and I.

B. The first year of the pretenure period establishes an experiential base. The second year provides for the major revisions. The third year shall result in a refined program growing out of the comparisons of the first two years' experience.

C. During the first year, each faculty member shall design appropriate learning-experience plans for at least two (2) courses (one course each of two semesters). These plans will be based upon self-instructional and other techniques, written behavioral objectives, and their associated evaluation procedures. Upon college approval, and concurrently, each faculty member will implement, manage, and evaluate student performance in relation to the designed learning experiences.

D. During the second year, the initial course designs will be refined. If any courses are canceled, however, new ones will be required. The faculty member may be asked to develop one additional course each semester of the second year.

E. A refined instructional program based on the comparisons of the first two years of experience will be developed during the third year of the pretenure period.

SECTION III. CLASSIFICATION AND PROMOTION

A. All appointees accepting initial contracts shall be classified as associate professor designate. Reappointment to the faculty of the college and a renewal of the contract shall be predicated on efficient performances during the period of the initial contract.

B. Upon completion of the pretenure period and the issuance of a tenure contract, faculty will be assigned academic rank and be eligible for subsequent promotion according to the following criteria:

  (1) *Instructor:* The following two criteria of efficiency are prerequisite for the rank of instructor:

   (a) The instructor will be responsible for designing, implementing, managing, and evaluating learning experiences for a minimum of 240 student credit hours per semester.

   (b) At least 60 per cent of the students enrolled in the instructor's classes at the time of registration will achieve stated objectives at a level satisfactory for transfer to a senior institution if in a transfer course, or, at a level satisfactory for employment if in an occupational course.

  (2) *Assistant Professor:* The following two criteria of efficiency are prerequisite for the rank of assistant professor:

   (a) The assistant professor will be responsible for designing, implementing, managing, and evaluating learning experiences for a minimum of 480 student credit hours per semester.

   (b) At least 70 per cent of the students enrolled in the assistant professor's classes at the time of registration will achieve stated objectives at a level satisfactory for transfer to a senior institution if in a transfer course, or, at a level satisfactory for employment if in an occupational course.

(3) *Associate Professor:* The following two criteria of efficiency are prerequisite for the rank of associate professor:

    (a) The associate professor will be responsible for designing, implementing, managing, and evaluating learning experiences for a minimum of 720 student credit hours per semester.

    (b) At least 80 per cent of the students enrolled in the associate professor's classes at the time of registration will achieve stated objectives at a level satisfactory for transfer to a senior institution if in a transfer course, or, at a level satisfactory for employment if in an occupational course.

(4) *Full Professor:* The following two criteria of efficiency are prerequisite for the rank of full professor:

    (a) The full professor will be responsible for designing, implementing, managing, and evaluating learning experiences for a minimum of 960 student credit hours per semester.

    (b) At least 90 per cent of the students enrolled in the full professor's classes at the time of registration will achieve stated objectives at a level satisfactory for transfer to a senior institution if in a transfer course, or, at a level satisfactory for employment if in an occupational course.

C. A faculty member in any rank may qualify for or attain any higher rank following any three academic years of performance at the higher level.

D. A reduction in rank for inefficiency will occur after three (3) consecutive academic years wherein the criteria for a given rank are not met; in the case of the instructor rank, the individual will be dismissed for inefficiency. Faculty members assigned three courses in a semester will be expected to meet the student hour criteria of the next lower academic rank. The criteria regarding achievement, however, will not be waived.

125

Appendix A

SECTION IV. COPYRIGHTS

The appointee does hereby agree and by the execution of this contract does hereby assign to the Passaic County College all right, title, and ownership in any and all publications, manuscripts, instructional systems, and tools developed, produced, or created during the course of his employment, excepting therefrom any of the above as may have been produced or created on the appointee's own time and/or materials; provided further, however, that the college shall at all times give credit to the appointee for authorship, notwithstanding the college's retention of all rights of sale and/or lease or reproduction of same.

B

Sample Policy on Accountability

WHEREAS, equal opportunity for all persons is a cherished American ideal;

WHEREAS, personal opportunity in the contemporary world is largely dependent upon competencies gained through the process of formal education;

WHEREAS, John Tyler Community College is a public institution existing for causing students to learn in accordance with their own goals and the needs of our society and economy;

WHEREAS, accountability for student learning is an accepted responsibility of the entire college community;

WHEREAS, the local board of John Tyler Community College is desirous of continuing the development of an instructional program that accommodates differential learning rates of students and produces measurable evidence of student learning;

NOW, THEREFORE, BE IT RESOLVED that the

1. college president shall periodically inform the local board of:
    (1) the success of students in attaining course objectives, including their attrition and failure rates;

    (2) the success of students in occupations assumed upon leaving the college, including the employer's perception of the value of the college's programs;

    (3) the success of students who transfer to other institutions;

    (4) the extent to which the programs of the college are attaining the stated aims of the college.

2. college community is encouraged to:

    (1) continue the development of an instructional program that accommodates differential learning rates of students and produces measurable evidence of student learning;

    (2) foster an "open and frank atmosphere" focused on enhancing the "teaching-learning climate" for which the college has been commended by the accrediting agency;

    (3) emphasize research-based planning for the continuing refinement of the instructional program to the end that college resources contribute maximally to opening the doorways of opportunities for students.

Questions for Presidential Candidates

The board should set the conditions for presidential leadership and then find a man who will accept total responsibility for such leadership. If possible the board should seek not simply an institutional administrator but an *educational leader* who is able and willing to be held as accountable for *student learning* as for his other responsibilities.

In an interview situation, one means to identify a man who is willing to accept responsibility for *student learning* is to ask him the right questions and tell him what is expected of him in the job. If the board only asks questions about buildings, budgets, previous experience, etc., it may expect that the man will respond in kind and not address himself directly to the central reason for the existence of the college: student learning in accordance with their own goals and the needs of our society and economy.

When the candidate is interviewed, that for which he is to be called to account can quickly be made known to him. If he is a flexible, dynamic sort, he will rise to the challenge; if not, it is better for all that it be known in advance. The man who becomes the new president must —if he is to be called *educational* leader—hold himself accountable for student learning and not leave student achievement to tradition and good intentions.

Sample Policy on Accountability

Following are a list of questions which may be helpful to the board to ask presidential candidates. By no means are these questions all that should be asked. They represent an attempt to give a new president some indications of the significant educational challenges facing John Tyler Community College.

1. Fact: The average test scores of new students entering John Tyler Community College are lower in all categories (math, English, natural science, social science) on an examination given nationwide than the average scores for all new students entering other Virginia community colleges.

Question: Will you assume responsibility for the design of programs which will accommodate students who enter the college unprepared for meeting the demands of college freshman work and assure that such programs are in fact successful in terms of student progression to higher levels of study and the number of students who stick with the program? Do you have any specific ideas as to how you would achieve this? Will you be willing to give a report on this to the board after each quarter?

2. Fact: Student performance on the job assumed after leaving the college is an important measure of the success of the college. The perception of the college held by leaders in industry, business, and the professions will have much influence on the development of the college.

Question: Will you periodically survey employers for information which will indicate how they perceive the college's programs and report the results of this survey information to the board?

3. Fact: It is a policy of the Virginia Community College System that faculty increases shall be on "merit." The policy does not define how merit shall be determined. Merit pay, when practiced, traditionally does not (or is unable to) base increases on student learning. The "systems approach to instruction" now being developed at John Tyler Community College provides the instructor with the means to demonstrate evidence of productivity in terms of student achievement. In its simplest form, this evidence can be final-examination papers which may be compared to the results of a test given to students at the beginning of the quarter.

Question: Will you assure that faculty members are held

accountable for student learning and that pay increases are based on student achievement insofar as feasible?

4. Fact: A community college has many different programs. Tyler has about twenty-five. Students are ordinarily not allowed to enter many programs without screening. The process of screening is crucial for student progression and achievement. Currently, the exclusion of students from programs of study for whatever sound reasons is a source of controversy on many campuses.

Question: Will you give attention to the bases used for placing students in different programs and report periodically the results to the board on this matter?

5. Fact: Higher education is essentially conservative and change does not come easily. Most professors are inclined to lecture as the predominant mode of instruction. Experimentation with and refinement of the instructional process is needed. Experimentation for its own sake is not the purpose, but rather experimentation based on a carefully developed plan for enhancing student learning.

Bibliography

ABELSON, R. P., and CARROLL, J. D. "Computer Simulation of Belief Systems." *American Behavioral Science,* 1965, *8.*

ALLEN, J. quoted in *The Washington Post,* March 30, 1970, p. A-2.

BANATHY, B. H. *Instructional Systems.* Belmont, Calif.: Fearon, 1968.

BASHAW, W. L. "The Effect of Community Junior Colleges on the Proportion of the Local Population Who Seek Higher Education." *The Journal of Educational Research,* Mar. 1965, *58.*

BLOCKER, C. E. and others. *The Two Year College: A Social Synthesis.* Englewood Cliffs, N.J.: Prentice-Hall, 1965.

BLOOM, B. S. "Learning for Mastery." In *Evaluation Comment.* Los Angeles: Center for the Study of Evaluation of Instructional Programs, University of California, 1968.

BLOOM, B. and others. *A Taxonomy of Educational Objectives: The Classification of Educational Goals. Handbook 1: Cognitive Domain.* New York: McKay, 1956.

BLOOM, B. S. and others. *Handbook on Formative and Summative Evaluation of Student Learning.* New York: McGraw-Hill, 1971.

BOSSONE, R. M. "Remedial English Instruction in California Public Junior Colleges: An Analysis and Evaluation of Current Practices." Sacramento, Calif.: California State Department of Education, 1966.

BROWN, H. S., and MAYHEW, L. B., *American Higher Education.* New York: Center for Applied Research in Education, 1965.

BRUNER, J. S. *The Process of Education.* New York: Random House, 1960.

BRUNER, J. S. *Toward a Theory of Instruction.* New York: Norton, 1966.

BRUNER, J. S. and others. *A Study of Thinking.* New York: Wiley, 1956.

BURTON, W. H. *Guidance of Learning Activities.* (3rd ed.) New York: Appleton-Century-Crofts, 1962.

BURTON, W. H. and others. *Education for Effective Thinking: An Introductory Text.* New York: Appleton-Century-Crofts, 1960.

CARLSON, R. O. "Barriers to Change in Public Schools." In *Change Processes in the Public Schools.* Eugene, Ore.: The Center for the Advanced Study of Educational Administration, University of Oregon, 1965.

CARROLL, J. A. "A Model of School Learning." *Teachers College Record,* 1963, *64.*

CHASE, F. S. "School Change in Perspective." In J. I. Goodlad (Ed.), *The Changing American School.* Chicago: University of Chicago Press, 1966.

CLARK, B. R. *The Open-Door College: A Case Study.* New York: McGraw-Hill, 1960.

COHEN, A. M. "Developing Specialists in Learning." *Junior College Journal,* Sept. 1966, *37.*

COHEN, A. M. *Dateline '79: Heretical Concepts for the Community College.* Beverly Hills, Calif.: Glencoe, 1969.

COHEN, A. M. *Objectives for College Courses.* Beverly Hills, Calif.: Glencoe, 1970.

COHEN, A. M., and BRAWER, F. B. *Focus on Learning: Preparing Teachers for the Two-Year College.* Occasional Report 11. Los Angeles: Junior College Leadership Program, University of California Graduate School of Education, 1968.

COHEN, A. M., and BRAWER, B. *Measuring Faculty Performance.* Washington, D.C.: American Association of Junior Colleges, 1969.

COHEN, A. M., and ROUECHE, J. E. *Institutional Administrator or Educational Leader?* Washington, D.C.: American Association of Junior Colleges, 1969.

Bibliography

COHEN, E. "Masters College Program." Final report to advisory board members and Union for Research and Experimentation in Higher Education Staff. Unpublished manuscript, Antioch College, Yellow Springs, Ohio, 1969.

COLE, W. G. "Breaking the Grade and Credit Mold." In G. L. Schwilck (Ed.), *The Challenge of Curricular Change*. New York: College Entrance Examination Board, 1966.

COLEMAN, J. S. *Equality of Educational Opportunity*. Washington, D.C.: Government Printing Office, 1966.

COMMITTEE FOR ECONOMIC DEVELOPMENT. "Innovations in Education: New Directions for the American School." Unpublished manuscript, 1968.

CROSS, K. P. *The Junior College Student: A Research Description*. Princeton, N.J.: Educational Testing Service, 1968.

CROSS, K. P. "The Junior College's Role in Providing Postsecondary Education for All." Berkeley: Center for Research and Development in Higher Education, University of California, and Educational Testing Service. 1969.

DALE, E. "Instructional Resources." In J. I. Goodlad (Ed.), *The Changing American School*. Chicago: University of Chicago Press, 1966.

D'AMICO, L. A., and BOKELMAN, R. W. "Tuition and Fee Charges in Public Junior Colleges, 1961–62." *Junior College Journal*, Sept. 1962, *33*.

DAVIES, D. "Newsmakers: Accountability." *College Management*, Feb. 1970, *5*.

Education Turnkey News. 1970, *1* (1).

ESBENSEN, T. "Writing Instructional Objectives." *Phi Delta Kappan*, Jan. 1967, *48*.

FEIGENBAUM, E. A. "The Simulation of Verbal Learning Behavior." In E. A. Feigenbaum and J. Feigenbaum (Eds.), *Computers and Thought*. New York: McGraw-Hill, 1963.

FLORIDA STATE DEPARTMENT OF EDUCATION, STATE JUNIOR COLLEGE ADVISORY BOARD. *Five Years of Progress: Florida's Community Junior Colleges*. Tallahassee, 1963.

FRIEDMAN, N. L. "Task Adaption Patterns of New Teachers." *Improving College and University Teaching*, Spring 1969, *17*.

GAGNE, R. M. "The Analysis of Instructional Objectives for the Design of Instruction." In R. Glaser (Ed.), *Teaching Machines and*

Bibliography

Programmed Learning II: Data and Directions. Washington, D.C.: National Education Association, 1965.

GARDNER, J. W. *Excellence: Can We Be Equal and Excellent Too?* New York: Harper and Row, 1960.

GARRISON, R. H. "What Students Want." *Improving College and University Teaching,* Summer 1969, *17.*

GLASER, R. "The Design of Instruction." In J. I. Goodlad (Ed.), *The Changing American School.* Chicago: University of Chicago Press, 1966.

GLASER, R. "Adapting the Elementary School Curriculum to Individual Performance." Princeton, N.J.: Educational Testing Service, 1968a.

GLASER, R. "Ten Untenable Assumptions of College Instruction." *Educational Record,* 1968b, *49*(2).

GLEAZER, E. J., JR. (Ed.) *American Junior Colleges.* Washington, D.C.: American Council on Education, 1963.

GLEAZER, E. J. *This Is the Community College.* Boston: Houghton Mifflin, 1969.

GLEAZER, E. J. "The Community College Issue of the 70's." *The Educational Record,* Winter 1970.

GOODLAD, J. I. "Where Precollege Reform Stands Today." In G. L. Schwilck, *The Challenge of Curricular Change.* New York: College Entrance Examination Board, 1966.

GOODLAD, J. I., and ANDERSON, R. H. *The Nongraded Elementary School.* New York: Harcourt Brace Jovanovich, 1959.

GORDON, E. W. *The Higher Education of the Disadvantaged.* Washington, D.C.: U.S. Office of Education, 1967.

GOW, J. S. and others. "Economic, Social, and Political Forces." In J. I. Goodlad (Ed.), *The Changing American School.* Chicago: University of Chicago Press, 1966.

GRIFFITHS, D. E. "Administrative Theory and Change in Organizations." In M. B. Miles (Ed.), *Innovation in Education.* New York: Teachers College, Columbia University, 1964.

HERRSCHER, B. R. *Implementing Individualized Instruction.* Houston: ArChem Publishers, 1970.

HILGARD, E. R., and BOWER, G. H. *Theories of Learning.* (3rd ed.) New York: Appleton-Century-Crofts, 1966.

HURLBURT, A. S. *State Master Plans for Community Colleges.* Washington, D.C.: American Association of Junior Colleges, 1969.

134

Bibliography

HUTCHINS, R. M. *The Learning Society*. New York: New American Library, 1968.

JENCKS, C. "New Breed of B.S.'s." *New Republic*, 1965, *153*.

JENCKS, C., and RIESMAN, D. *The Academic Revolution*. Garden City, N.Y.: Doubleday, 1968.

JOHNSON, B. L. *New Directions for Instruction in the Junior College*. Occasional Report 7. Los Angeles: Junior College Leadership Program, University of California Graduate School of Education, 1965.

JOHNSON, B. L. (Ed.) *Systems Approaches to Curriculum and Instruction in the Open-Door College*. Occasional Report 9. Los Angeles: Junior College Leadership Program, University of California Graduate School of Education, 1967.

JOHNSON, B. L. *Islands of Innovation Expanding: Changes in the Community College*. Beverly Hills, Calif.: Glencoe, 1969.

JOHNSON, S., and JOHNSON, R. *Developing Individualized Instructional Materials*. Palo Alto, Calif.: Westinghouse Learning Corporation, 1970.

KEMP, J. E. "A Plan for Curriculum and Instructional Development." Unpublished manuscript, Audio-Visual Services, San Jose State College, 1969.

KOLB, W. L. "A College Plan Designed for Flexibility." In G. L. Schwilck (Ed.), *The Challenge of Curricular Change*. New York: College Entrance Examination Board, 1966.

KNOELL, D. *People Who Need College*. Washington: American Association of Junior Colleges, 1970.

KNOELL, D. M., and MEDSKER, L. L. *From Junior to Senior College*. Washington, D.C: American Council on Education, 1966.

KRATHWOHL, D. R. and others. *A Taxonomy of Educational Objectives: The Classification of Educational Goals. Handbook 2: Affective Domain*. New York: McKay, 1964.

LEE, G. C. "The Changing Role of the Teacher." In J. I. Goodlad (Ed.), *The Changing American School*. Chicago: University of Chicago Press, 1966.

LEONARD, G. B. *Education and Ecstasy*. New York: Dell, 1968.

LOMBARD, J. W. "Preparing Better Classroom Tests." *The Science Teacher*, Oct. 1965, *32*.

MC INTYRE, C., and STUART, J. "Financial Assistance Programs for

Bibliography

California College and University Students." Staff Report 67-13. Sacramento, Calif.: Coordinating Council for Higher Education, 1967.

MAGER, R. F. *Preparing Instructional Objectives.* Belmont, Calif.: Fearon, 1962.

MAGER, R. F. *Developing Attitude Toward Learning.* Belmont, Calif.: Fearon, 1968.

MEDSKER, L. L., and TILLERY, D. *Breaking the Access Barrier.* New York: McGraw-Hill, 1971.

MEDSKER, L., and TRENT, J. *Factors Affecting College Attendance of High School Graduates from Varying Socioeconomic and Ability Levels.* Berkeley: Center for Research and Development in Higher Education, University of California, 1965.

MICHAEL, L. S. "The High School's Changing Task." In G. I. Schwilck (Ed.), *The Challenge of Curricular Change.* New York: College Entrance Examination Board, 1966.

MILES, M. B. "Educational Innovation: The Nature of the Problem." In M. B. Miles (Ed.), *Innovation in Education.* New York: Teachers College Press, 1964.

MILLER, G. A. and others. *Plans and the Structure of Behavior.* New York: Holt, Rinehart, and Winston, 1960.

MINK, O. *The Behavior Change Process.* New York: Harper and Row, 1970.

MOONEY, R. L. "Groundwork for Creative Research." *The American Psychologist,* Sept. 1954, 9.

MOONEY, R. L. "Creation and Teaching." *Bulletin of the Bureau of School Service,* 1963, 35.

MOONEY, R. L. "Creation in the Classroom Setting." Columbus: Ohio State University, 1966.

MORGAN, R. *Psychology: An Individualized Course.* Palo Alto, Calif.: Westinghouse Learning Corporation, 1970.

MORRISON, H. C. *The Practice of Teaching in the Secondary School.* Chicago: University of Chicago Press, 1926.

MORT, P. R. "Studies in Educational Innovation." In M. D. Miles (Ed.), *Innovation in Education.* New York: Teachers College Press, 1964.

MORT, P. R., and CORNELL, F. G. *American Schools in Transition.* New York: Bureau of Publications, Teachers College, Columbia University. 1941.

136

Bibliography

NATIONAL SOCIETY FOR THE STUDY OF EDUCATION. *The Public Junior College*. Chicago: University of Chicago Press, 1956.

NEWBURN, H. K. "The Board Meets the President." *Junior College Journal,* Nov. 1964, *35.*

POPHAM, J. W. *The Teacher Empiricist: A Curriculum and Instruction Supplement.* Los Angeles: Tinnon-Brown, 1965.

PRESIDENT'S COMMISSION ON NATIONAL GOALS. *Goals for America.* Englewood Cliffs, N.J.: Prentice-Hall, 1961.

RAUH, M. A. *The Trusteeship of Colleges and Universities.* New York: McGraw-Hill, 1969.

ROMINE, B. H. "Field Development: A Procedure for Change in Educational Systems." Durham: National Laboratory for Higher Education, 1969.

ROUECHE, J. E. *Salvage, Redirection, or Custody?* Washington, D.C.: American Association of Junior Colleges, 1968.

ROUECHE, J. E., BAKER, G. A., III, and BROWNELL, R. L. *Accountability and the Community College.* Washington, D.C.: American Association of Junior Colleges, 1971.

ROUECHE, J. E., and HERRSCHER, B. R. "A Learning-Oriented System of Instruction." *Junior College Journal,* Oct. 1970.

SHUMSKY, A. *In Search of Teaching Style.* New York: Appleton-Century-Crofts, 1965.

SIMON, H. A. "Scientific Discovery and the Psychology of Problem-Solving." In M. Wertheimer (Ed.), *Productive Thinking.* New York: Harper and Row, 1959.

SKINNER, B. F. "The Science of Learning and the Art of Teaching." *Harvard Educational Review,* 1954, *24.*

SUPPES, P. "The Uses of Computers in Education." *Scientific American,* 1966, *215.*

TENDLER, M., and WILSON, R. E. *Community College Trustees: Responsibilities and Opportunities.* Washington, D.C.: American Association of Junior Colleges, 1970.

THELEN, H. A. "Reading for Inquiry." *Controversial Issues in Reading and Promising Solution: Proceedings of the Annual Conference on Reading,* 1961, *23,* Chap. 3.

THORNTON, J. W. *The Community Junior College.* (2nd ed.) New York: Wiley, 1966.

TRENT, J. W., and MEDSKER, L. L. *Beyond High School.* San Francisco: Jossey-Bass, 1968.

Bibliography

TYLER, R. *Basic Principles of Curriculum and Instruction: Syllabus for Education 305.* Chicago: University of Chicago Press, 1950.

TYLER, R. W. "The Behavioral Sciences and the Schools." In J. I. Goodlad (Ed.), *The Changing American School.* Chicago: University of Chicago Press, 1966.

WASHBURN, B. "Media in Instructional Packages." Durham, N.C.: National Laboratory for Higher Education, 1971.

WEBSTER, A. *Webster's Seventh New Collegiate Dictionary.* Springfield, Mass.: Merriam, 1969.

WILLINGHAM, W. W., and NURHAN, F. "Transfer Students, Who's Moving from Where to Where, and What Determines Who's Admitted." *College Board Review,* Summer 1969, *72.*

WRINKLE, W. L. *Improving Marking and Reporting Practices.* New York: Holt, Rinehart, and Winston, 1950.

Index

139

Index